Alexandria

PORTRAIT OF A CITY

Alexandria

PORTRAIT OF A CITY

text by BETH S. OFFENBACKER · photography by NINA TISARA & STEVEN A. HALPERSON

Acknowledgments

Layout, design, and production of this publication
by Platinum Publishing Company, Inc.
7 Old Solomons Island Road
Annapolis, Maryland 21401
(410) 224-1111/(800) 783-1238

Text ©1997 by Beth S. Offenbacker.
Photography ©1997 by Nina Tisara
and Steven A. Halperson.

1st Printing, 1997.

ISBN 1-890291-05-6

Color separation and film preparation by
Platinum Publishing Company, Inc.

Sponsors

ABAN Computers
Alexandria Chamber of Commerce
Alexandria City Public Schools
Alexandria Economic Development Partnership, Inc.
American Association of Colleges of Pharmacy
City of Alexandria
Club Managers Association of America
Commonwealth Atlantic Properties, Inc.
Eakin/Youngentob Associates
Executive Club Suites
The George Washington University
Hoffman Management
Holland Engineering
Inova Mount Vernon Hospital
Jane's Information Group
The Mark Winkler Company
Mount Comfort Cemetery
The National Association of Chain Drug Stores
National Association of Temporary
    and Staffing Services
Northern Virginia Community College
Potomac Partners, Inc.
The Restaurant Cruise Ship Dandy
    and The Potomac Riverboat Company
Society for Human Resource Management
Stabler-Leadbeater Apothecary Museum
Stevens Reed Curcio & Company
Time Life Inc.
Virginia-American Water Company
Washington Gas

Alexandria

PORTRAIT OF A CITY

Mayor Kerry J. Donley
FOREWORD

It is an honor and a privilege to introduce
you to The Economic History of Alexandria.
I am proud, both as Mayor and as an
Alexandrian, to laud the rich history and
crowning achievements of this diverse and
dynamic community.

The growth and evolution of the City of Alexandria, from a colonial seaport to an innovative technology center through nearly 250 years, is a model for historians, economists and anthropologists alike. For the historian, Alexandria represents a scale model of the best this great nation has to offer. For the economist, Alexandria serves as a case study of how government, business, civic organizations and neighbors work together to create a city that promotes success and celebrates a good quality of life. For the anthropologist, Alexandria is a study in diversity, and an exercise in how a community can pool its best resources to create a synergistic environment.

The City of Alexandria has witnessed myriad changes in its 250-year history. From a tiny trading post on the Potomac River during colonial times, Alexandria grew to a bustling port city. This commercial center was fre-

quented by some of this nation's founding fathers, including George Washington to whom Alexandrians boast a special link.

Alexandria flourished and adapted to the changing economic face of America, while thriving as a tourism and cultural center. Today, Alexandria is host to more than 300 associations. The City is also a burgeoning locus for cutting-edge technology, placing second as a technology center in Northern Virginia's "Silicon Dominion."

This portrait of Alexandria's economic history, produced by our Chamber of Commerce, represents both pride and prophecy. As we reflect on our grand history and accomplishments, we look to the future with the same courage and confidence our forebears brought to our seaport city. We invite you to become a part of us.

A Powerful Center of
BUSINESS

Fostered by a strong pro-business atmosphere in a historical setting, the City of Alexandria is Northern Virginia's glistening star. During the 1990's, the City ranked in the top 2 percent of all U.S. counties and independent cities in a variety of desirable categories, including educational attainment, income, mobility and race and diversity.

Right page: American Trucking Association's headquarters building.

Alexandria

Alexandria was founded in 1749 as a seaport by Scottish merchants, and it has since maintained a strong presence as a focal point of commercial activity in Virginia. Known as George Washington's hometown, Alexandria is where he and fellow patriots held meetings and attended church and the theater during the formative years of the American Revolution. His noted estate, Mount Vernon, is just 8 miles south of the City.

Alexandria is complemented by the beauty of the Virginia countryside and the historic charm of the area. Businesses, families and individuals from around the country and across the world have made this vibrant and growing community of 118,000 people and 6,500 businesses their chosen place, for work and for play.

The 11th densest city in the nation, Alexandria still maintains a special charm that is not lost on residents or visitors. More than 20 years ago, urban renewal projects, stimulated by concerned Alexandrians from the business and residential communities, revitalized the city's downtown Historic District.

Left page: 1. Mount Vernon, George Washington's famous home. 2. Colonial troops at Mount Vernon. 3. A street musician plays for King Street shoppers. *Right page:* The beautiful Virginia countryside.

Alexandria

Located near the center of the metropolitan Washington area, Alexandria is a vibrant hub for businesses, technology firms, non-profit organizations, professional associations and federal agencies.

Retail businesses and restaurants have also found Alexandria's business climate greatly to their liking, due to the high concentration of businesses and a residential median household income of $50,120. Truly, Alexandria is blessed with a diverse economic base, employing more than 83,000 people within the City's 15.75 square miles.

Nationally, Alexandria is one of 17 cities and 14 counties in the United States to hold an AAA bond rating from both of Wall Street's top rating agencies, Standard & Poor's and Moody's Investors Service. Alexandria's debt per capita is the lowest and its 1997 property tax rate of $1.07 per $100 of assessed value is among the lowest in Northern Virginia.

Downtown Alexandria is only two miles from 19 major airlines at National Airport and just a just five-mile drive to Washington, D.C.. The Pentagon, home of the U.S. Defense Department, is four miles away. City firms value the proximity to the Federal Government and Northern Virginia's own "Silicon Dominion," which stretches from Alexandria as far west as Loudoun County.

Left page: 1. One of Alexandria's many antique shops. 2. Alexandria's view of National Airport and the Capitol. Right page: 1. The Food Court on the pier in Old Town. 2. Egerton Gardens, an antique and gift shop on South Washington Street.

Alexandria

Gateway to Business

Area residents and visitors can travel to Alexandria and other Washington metropolitan communities by using any of the city's multiple public transportation venues. Bus service includes Metrobus, Alexandria City's DASH and the Fairfax County Connector service.

Alexandria also has four Metrorail stations, an AMTRAK train station and rail service via the Virginia Railway Express, which serves outlying communities in Fairfax, Prince William and Stafford counties. For commuters or visitors who prefer to drive to the city, parking is easy to find and costs are extremely competitive without sacrificing location or quality urban environment. A growing number of Alexandria businesses, for example, participate in the Alexandria Chamber of Commerce's *Park Alexandria* program, which offers discount parking to City visitors at public garages throughout Old Town.

A strong network of intra- and interstate highways and parkways offer Alexandria visitors, residents and workers many choices. The city has several interchanges with the major transportation link of I-495/ I-95, an east coast interstate artery that connects Maine to Florida. Nearby, Virginia's I-395 offers intrastate access to residents and businesses on Alexandria's West End. And, southeastern and northeastern sectors of adjacent Fairfax County are accessible via the scenic George Washington Memorial Parkway.

Improvements being made to the Woodrow Wilson Bridge, National Airport's expanded terminal and other infrastructure in and around the City of Alexandria will improve the flow of traffic while allowing for planned growth. The new Eisenhower Interchange to I-495 (the Capital Beltway) will offer improved commuter access to the Eisenhower Avenue corridor.

*Left page: 1. George Washington Parkway. 2. Alexandria's Amtrak Station, at the foot of Shuter's Hill. **Right page:** King Street Metro at night.*

Alexandria

The Many Business Communities of Alexandria

Alexandria's business community is as diverse as its people and stretches across the breadth of the City.

The Old Town business community is the historical heart of the City and has more than 200 speciality and import shops. Dozens of fine restaurants also dot the area and provide for every taste imaginable, from Greek, French and Japanese, to Thai, Italian, Spanish and American. These shops and restaurants are popular lunchtime retreats for professionals with offices in the area.

Old Town is also full of nearly 1,000 buildings with Georgian, Greek Revival, Federal and other architectural styles, many of which have been preserved and restored as businesses, museums and homes. In fact, the Old Town portion of the City has been named a National Landmark by the National Register of Historic Places.

Left page: 1. The Winterthur Museum Store. 2. The Chart House Restaurant is a big draw for al fresco dining.
Right page: 1. One of Alexandria's few remaining cobblestone streets. 2. Alexandria's unique beauty at night.

Alexandria

While the historic district resides squarely along the Potomac River to the east and ends at Harvard Street to the west, Old Town's business community stretches beyond it, from the townhouse-style office complexes on South Washington Street north to Canal Plaza's mid- and high-rise buildings. Old Town's western edge extends to the King Street Metro Station, and it is this area of Old Town, in particular, that has experienced new growth in recent years as the City flourishes as a business center.

Another, among Alexandria's quickly expanding business communities, is Potomac West. New economic development is giving rise to upscale eateries and antique shops, travel agencies and florists. A coffee house and a number of ethnic restaurants, artistic alliances, small businesses, professional associations, churches and non-profit organizations reside "along the Avenue," as the 1.5 mile stretch of Mount Vernon Avenue is known in local parlance.

Left page: 1. An arch adorning Mount Vernon Avenue's Shops. 2. The Saturday morning Farmer's Market in Del Ray. Right page: 1. RT's Restaurant, a Mount Vernon Avenue institution. 2. Mt. Vernon Avenue offer a variety of goods and services.

Alexandria

West End Alexandria, often called Landmark, is a wonderful mix of old and new. Alexandrians and people from all over the metropolitan area travel to the West End for shopping at the 150-store Landmark Mall. Abundant ethnic and family restaurants, special services and medical offices are also located in the vicinity. Clustered near the mall on Van Dorn and Pickett streets are dozens of other retail shops, purveying everything from hardware to home supplies, from computers to cake decorations.

The West End is the site of Northern Virginia Community College, which soon will house the $9 million Rachel M. Schlesinger Concert Hall and Arts Center. This 1,000-seat theater will be the new home of the Alexandria Symphony Orchestra and will serve as a shared-use facility between the college, Alexandria and the neighboring jurisdiction of Arlington. Other West End development includes Cameron Station, a former Army base which is being redeveloped into a mixed-use community of retail shops, town homes and mid-rise condominium apartments.

Left page: 1. *A children's puppet show at Landmark Shopping Center.* 2. *The fun of the xylophone – a child takes a lesson from an Alexandria Symphony musician.*
Right page: 1. *Facing the Landmark area, on Duke Street.* 2. *The Bisdorf Building at Northern Virginia Community College in the West End.*

Alexandria

Eisenhower Avenue is one of the most exciting new corridors of the city. Site of the Carlyle condominium complex, the Time-Life headquarters, the new Albert V. Bryan Federal Courthouse, the Society of Human Resource Management and a number of other business and federal organizations, Eisenhower Avenue is a dynamic community anchored by its many high-technology businesses. The corridor's reasonable prices and open spaces have attracted townhome communities and build-to-suit commercial development. Within its boundaries exists three connections to I-495, the region's Capital Beltway.

Potomac Yard in the northeastern end of the City is another developing business community. Formerly owned by the Richmond, Fredericksburg and Potomac Railroad Company, the 300 acre property is developing as a mixed-use community with commercial offices, retail stores, hotels, townhomes and multi-family dwellings.

The northern portion of the property consists of a 600,000 square-foot retail center. Residents and area office workers will have a large variety of retail stores at which to shop, anchored by a Target store, Barnes and Noble bookstore and HomePlace. Additional retail businesses include clothing, accessories, sporting goods and office supplies, among others. Potomac Yard will offer opportunities for entertainment including a 16-screen, all-stadium seating cinema located directly behind the shopping center.

Left page: The Time-Life Building on Duke Street in Old Town.
Right page: The Carlyle, one of the City's newest luxury condominiums, located near the Time-Life Building.

Alexandria

A Diverse Real Estate Market Meets Every Need

A quality office market with diverse purchase, lease, build-to-suit and condominium opportunities has been especially appealing to businesses and associations that are considering Alexandria as a candidate in the site selection process.

Formerly housed in multi-tenant structures in other cities, many Alexandria-based businesses and associations gain a higher profile, yet fixed overhead costs, all within their own buildings. Alexandria makes these options most attractive, offering low interest, tax-exempt revenue bond financing for building purchase or lease for 501(c)(3) and 501(c)(6) corporations.

A consistently low office vacancy rate is testimony to Alexandria's appeal in the metropolitan region. Yet a wide variety of build-to-suit opportunities remain. At 7.9 percent, the vacancy rate is among the lowest in the Washington D.C. area.

Families also look to Alexandria for housing in a comfortable and attractive urban setting. Homes in Alexandria are considered affordable at an average cost of $177,640. Single-family homes, condominiums and apartments are prevalent, with more than 61,753 housing units in the market. About 48 percent of the households in Alexandria are rentals, with an average monthly rent of $716 for a one-bedroom unit. Condominiums occupy another 22 percent of the market, with the remaining 31 percent consisting of single-family structures.

Left page: 1. Canal Center, an office complex located on the waterfront in northern Old Town. 2. Embassy Suites takes on a warm glow at sunset. Right page: 1, 2. Architectural detail of the Canal Center complex. 3. The Mark Winkler Office Building and Radisson Mark Plaza Hotel, at dusk. 4. A West End condominium.

Alexandria's Labor Force:
PROFESSIONAL & PROFICIENT

A highly skilled labor force is a significant component of any business community. Employers rely on these competent workers to fill vacated positions as well as to support the organization's ability to effectively respond to market changes.

Firms in the Washington region, and in Alexandria, in particular, have a superb pool of candidates from which to choose. Known for the advanced education of its residents, the area has the most highly educated work force of any metropolitan market in the country. An impressive 40 percent of the population aged 25 and older possess baccalaureate degrees, and nearly 17 percent hold graduate and professional degrees. This strong base of talent, in both Alexandria and the metropolitan Washington area, is a tremendous resource for both public and private employers.

***Right page:** Advanced education makes Alexandria's workforce one of the most impressive in the country.*

Alexandria

Major Employers Choose Alexandria

Large employers are attracted to Alexandria for many reasons, among them proximity to Washington, reasonable costs, a skilled labor pool, and, of course, the grace of the City itself.

Private City-based organizations that employ significant numbers of persons include Alexandria Hospital, the Institute for Defense Analyses, the Pentagon Federal Credit Union, Giant Food, DynCorp, Boat Owners Association of America, the Center for Naval Analyses, Safeway Stores, the Radisson Plaza Hotel, Time-Life and Veda, Inc.

Large public employers in Alexandria include a number of federal, regional and local organizations. Among them are the U.S. Department of Agriculture, U.S. Postal Service, U.S. Treasury Department, Northern Virginia Community College, Washington Metro Area Transit Authority, Alexandria Public Schools and the City of Alexandria.

Left page: 1. The Radisson Mark Plaza Hotel is a popular place for conferences and social events. 2. The Pentagon Federal Credit Union, also headquartered in the City.
Right page: 1. Giant Food, one of Alexandria's major employers. 2. Exterior of the BOAT/U.S. Building, one of 300 trade associations based in Alexandria.

Alexandria

A Prominent Association Community

Alexandria has drawn a significant number of professional associations because of its close proximity to Washington, D.C. and its competitive lease/land costs and low tax rates.

The nation's fourth largest center for trade and professional associations-preceded only by Washington, D.C., New York and Chicago-Alexandria is the headquarters location for 300 associations varying from two- or three-person offices with annual budgets in the $100,000 to $250,000 range to extensive staffs and multi-million dollar operations.

Left page: 1. Printing Industries of America headquarters in Old Town. 2. The American Optometric Association on Prince Street. Right page: 1. Ben Franklin greets visitors outside the Printing Industries of America building. 2. Business in Alexandria is always done with a smile.

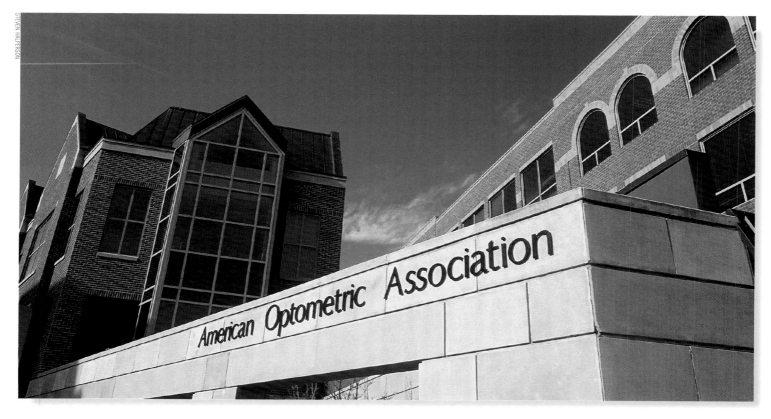

Alexandria

Training Tomorrow's Business Leaders

The educational foundation of a community is an important indicator of its future growth and success. The staff of the Alexandria City Public Schools has created a quality learning environment for the City's 10,000 primary and secondary students that prepares them for the challenges of both today and tomorrow's world. It is a school system and a student body that value differences while building unity, for this diverse student population speaks 44 native languages and represents 69 birth countries.

Well-known for its small class size and its program for gifted and talented students, Alexandria has embraced the future with its Technology Initiative. This four-year program allows children to take advantage of the latest in technological advances, including networked CD-ROM research resources, distance learning opportunities and in-school video production facilities. The Alexandria business community acknowledges the important role that education plays in training tomorrow's citizens and employees. It has become an integral partner with the school system in its Technology Initiative, in curriculum development, in technical training programs, in mentoring and other instructional initiatives.

Fifty Alexandria-based organizations have adopted schools within the City, culminating in the donation of more than 50,000 hours of volunteer service. Partnership volunteers support the children who attend Alexandria's 17 elementary and secondary schools. The Chamber of Commerce annually recognizes outstanding educators as part of its efforts to support education in the City.

Alexandria's private schools are another resource for area residents. From Bishop Ireton to St. Stephen's and St. Agnes School, from the Alexandria Country Day School to Episcopal High School, the City's private schools have excellent reputations.

*Left page: A class at Hammond Elementary School. **Right page:** 1. The Episcopal High School library, West Braddock Road. 2. Computers are a strong part of the curriculum in the City schools. 3. St. Stephen-St. Agnes School.*

Alexandria

Post-Secondary Training and Education

Adult students often look to Alexandria's many institutions of advanced learning for post-secondary training and education.

The Alexandria campus of Northern Virginia Community College in the West End offers more than 130 programs of study, serving as a community focal point for educational programs, business meetings and public forums. Its comprehensive curriculum includes programs in a variety of disciplines, from business administration to graphic design, from computer science to foreign languages.

The private Strayer College is another community educational resource for students seeking a business-oriented education. Offering a complete range of post-graduate, baccalaureate and associate degrees in addition to diploma programs, Strayer students can major in 14 different disciplines. Strayer's degree programs include business administration, economics, information systems and marketing, among others. The school's Alexandria location on Eisenhower Avenue is part of a 10-site campus.

Left page: 1. An art student at Northern Virginia Community College. Right page: 1. Strayer College's Alexandria campus. 2. Students have access to the latest technology in the library of Northern Virginia Community College.

Alexandria

For those seeking advanced degree programs, George Washington University's Alexandria Graduate Education Center, conveniently located across the street from the King Street Metro Station, offers nine master's degree programs. The center is part of the renowned George Washington University, based in the District of Columbia.

The Virginia Polytechnic Institute and State University, based in Blacksburg, Virginia, also has a presence in the City. Housed in a renovated turn-of-the-century schoolhouse on Prince Street, students use the metropolitan Washington region as a resource laboratory for research and design, drawing upon facilities such as the Smithsonian Institution, the American Institute of Architects and the National Building Museum.

Another specialized institution of higher learning in Alexandria is the Virginia Theological Seminary, one of the accredited seminaries of the Episcopal Church. Since 1823, the school has prepared men and women for ministries around the world. The seminary has one of the premier theological libraries of the Mid-Atlantic region, and offers opportunities for internships and cross-cultural missions.

Left page: 1. *George Washington University's Alexandria Graduate Education Center, near the King Street Metro Station.* 2. *Virginia Theological Seminary on Seminary Road.* ***Right page:*** *A small group discussion at the Alexandria Graduate Education Center.*

Alexandria

High-Tech Training for a High-Tech Workforce

Computer skills are a must for the technological age in which we live. The Computer Learning Center, TESST Technology Institute and Northern Virginia Community College all offer an array of computer and technical skills classes for adults at reasonable prices that fit a variety of schedules.

The Computer Learning Center provides advanced-level technical training as well as general education courses that provide students with a well-balanced educational experience that supports and complements existing technical knowledge and work skills.

TESST Technology Institute offers classroom instruction and practical, hands-on-training in a number of high-tech fields. The school's highly successful job placement program serves as a valuable resource to area employers.

Left page: 1. *A technician and an intern working together at Jones Communications.* 2. *Working on equipment at VSE lab.* **Right page:** 1. *Computer software training at Productivity Point.* 2. *TESST Technology Institute.*

Alexandria

A Vibrant Trade Industry

The City's trade industry is prominent, reflecting a considerable number of professions and industries. From plumbers and electricians to roofers and construction personnel, workers and the organizations that employ them are housed within Alexandria. These skilled crafts persons offer organizations in the City and surrounding jurisdictions quality handiwork second to none.

High Demand, Low Unemployment

A vibrant local economy has kept the jobless rate in Alexandria at a low 3.2 percent. Coupled with the thriving regional economy, the City's strong business climate benefits from a skilled talent pool from which to draw to meet the changing needs of their particular industries. These dynamics of the local economy in turn have driven the profits of area businesses to record levels, and have sustained continued growth in recent years. Low unemployment has created a stable base for businesses and residents, and, as a result, allowed the City government and Alexandria businesses to pursue a number of programs and community reinvestment projects that have made Alexandria the vibrant center of commerce it is today.

Left page: 1. Masons working hard to restore a wall in Old Town. 2. Both businesses and residents benefit from Alexandria's low unemployment rate. *Right page:* Sculpture outside Sheet Metal Workers Pension Fund Building.

An Innovative Climate for
BUSINESS

Pro-business and accessible City officials, business owners and residents work together to maintain the quality of life and safe environment that have attracted hundreds of national trade and professional associations, multinational corporations and technology firms to Alexandria.

It is this unique sense of a balanced community that makes the City of Alexandria stand apart from others in the region. Businesses and residents are encouraged to become involved in the process of making Alexandria an even better place in which to live and work.

One example of this is the State of Virginia's declaration of the Potomac West area on Mount Vernon Avenue an Enterprise Zone. The Enterprise Zone makes businesses located along the 1.5 mile strip eligible for special tax incentives in exchange for the businesses "reinvesting" in the surrounding neighborhood and its residents. Qualifying businesses can apply for substantial state tax credits and grants. The Enterprise Zone serves as a unique enclave for small business development and has been instrumental in the creation of more than 300 new jobs in its first two years.

Right page: Shoppers strolling along lower King Street.

Alexandria

An Unifying Force for Alexandria Business

Known as *the* voice for Alexandria business, the Alexandria Chamber of Commerce plays a crucial role in advocating a productive and profitable business climate for City-based corporations, non-profits and associations.

Governed by a 29-member Board of Directors, the chamber has served as a unifying force for the Alexandria business community for nearly a century. Its value lies in the many quality business programs and services it consistently delivers to its 1,000 member companies. The chamber's established reputation as a strong advocate for the business community serves the interests of Alexandria businesses at the City Council, regional, state and federal levels. It also conducts business development programs, supports small businesses and recruits large firms in an effort to expand the employment base of the City.

The chamber serves as a vital hub for professional development and business growth among City businesses and organizations. It sponsors a wide variety of educational, advocacy, networking and outreach efforts, including monthly Professional Networking breakfasts and receptions, a Small and Minority Business Fair, the Legislative Liaison program, the annual State of the City breakfast and the Governor's Luncheon.

In addition, the chamber sponsors a number of awards luncheons throughout the year, which honor police, fire, sheriff and rescue workers, educators and leading technology businesses, as well as outstanding small businesses in the City.

Left page: 1. Chamber staff and members interact at a Land Use Committee meeting. 2. Chamber mixers are an effective way to network as well as have a great time.
Right page: Rebecca Buckbee receives the Award of Excellence in Education.

Alexandria

Cultivating New and Existing Businesses

Recognizing the need to cultivate business growth in the City, a Small Business Development Center was established in the City in 1996. It is operated by the State of Virginia, the business community and the City in conjunction with The George Washington University, which provides staff and space for the center in addition to other in-kind services.

The SBDC was created as a result of the concerted efforts of City and state officials, The George Washington University, the Alexandria Chamber of Commerce, the Small & Minority Task Force, Alexandria Economic Development Partnership, Inc., and the U.S. Small Business Administration.

Its mission is to reinforce the goals of the Virginia Small Business Development Center network by assisting existing and potential businesses in Alexandria with improvements in management skills, productivity, and the business' ability to generate profits. These goals are realized by providing one-on-one small business counseling, training and information and referral services.

The center offers specialized business planning for technology firms, minority and women-owned small businesses, and retail operations as well as programs for businesses seeking to develop an international presence and the use of electronic commerce. All services are free except for small fees for workshops.

Access to various software packages, the World Wide Web, computers and computer-related training classes are available for new and existing businesses at the SBDC, located near the King Street Metro station in the George Washington University Alexandria Graduate Education Center.

*Left page: 1. SCORE counseling at the Small Business Development Center, located at the George Washington University. 2. The George Washington University Alexandria Graduate Education Center offers many computer training classes. **Right page:** M.B.A. students from George Washington University's Graduate Education Center counsel a local small business owner.*

Alexandria

A Public/Private Economic Development Effort

The Alexandria Economic Development Partnership, Inc., is a public/private partnership established in 1981 between the City of Alexandria and the Alexandria business community. This 501(c)(6) corporation is funded through an appropriation by City Council and investments made by individual businesses within and around the City. The partnership is governed by a public/private Board of Directors that is chaired by Alexandria's mayor.

The partnership has been instrumental over the past two decades in the development of a number of community resources, including the Alexandria Graduate Education Center of the George Washington University, the establishment of the Potomac West Enterprise Zone, a partnership with a local bank to administer a $100 million pooled loan program and the team effort to secure the Alexandria Small Business Development Center.

In the mid-1980s, the partnership's economic development efforts attracted hundreds of associations to Alexandria in a concerted marketing effort. It also developed an association executive's guide to Virginia and Alexandria laws and taxes, and developed a campus for national and professional associations that features expanded services and facilities as well as savings.

As a result of its efforts, the Greater Washington Society of Association Executives recognized the partnership with its Distinguished Service Award. The award is presented each year to the organization that has "contributed most extensively to the visibility and viability of national associations in Greater Washington."

Left page: The Hooff building gets a face lift. **Right page:** *A grove of trees provide shade to office workers at Mark Center.*

Alexandria

Promoting and Supporting Alexandria Tourism

The non-profit Alexandria Convention and Visitors Association (ACVA) provides assistance to tourists and meeting planners alike.

Meeting planners enjoy the ACVA's one-stop shopping approach, as it can arrange appointments, itineraries and site visits as well as make referrals to hospitality services and meeting facilities. The association also provides lists of local entertainers, historic reenactors, costumed guides, Scottish pipe bands and cultural and historic theme lecturers.

Tourists can visit the ACVA's Ramsay House Visitors Center on lower King Street, open every day except Thanksgiving, Christmas and New Year's Day. The center offers free parking passes, assists with historic site tickets, and provides brochures featuring area museums, shops, galleries, restaurants, hotels and attractions.

*Left page: 1. An 18th century period costumed guide greets children in Market Square, outside City hall. 2. The Ramsay House Visitor's Center at King and North Fairfax streets in Old Town. **Right page:** Bag pipers march as part of the St. Patrick's Day parade.*

Alexandria

Lauding Alexandria's Technology Firms

Recognizing technology firms as a prominent component of the Alexandria business community, the Alexandria City Council designates the second week of March as the annual Technology Achievement Week.

Sponsored by the City of Alexandria, the Alexandria Chamber of Commerce and the Alexandria Economic Development Partnership, Inc., this event promotes the City's 164 technology businesses and their technological innovations.

Technology Achievement Week activities include an awards program for finalists for the Alexandria Technology Achievement Awards, acknowledgment and proclamation for the award winners by the Alexandria City Council, and special presentations and technology displays at the Chamber of Commerce Professional Networking Breakfast.

A new Technology Council, coordinated by the Alexandria Chamber of Commerce, will continue to integrate these firms into the fabric of our unique and growing community.

Left page: Antennas at Jones Communications in Alexandria's West End.

Alexandria

Outlook for the Immediate Future

Alexandria is in the midst of progressive growth as the new millennium begins. New office development, growing technology and service businesses, and trade associations with expanding missions all have looked to the City as a place where business can be conducted pleasantly and with a competitive cost of operations.

Recognizing the importance of maintaining quality of life for its business residents, the City works closely with state officials and organizations such as the Alexandria Chamber of Commerce to ensure that plans and initiatives properly balance the needs of the business community with those of residents and other constituencies.

Left page: 1. Residential construction. 2. Woodrow Wilson Bridge's draw bridge, on Alexandria's southwest border. Right page: Commercial construction underway signaling Alexandria's continued growth.

Alexandria's Enchanting
ATTRACTIONS

The picturesque Alexandria waterfront is an irresistible attraction to both residents and visitors. On the shores of the Potomac River, Alexandria imparts a variety of options for tourists, including a cruise ship that docks in Alexandria several times each August. Dinner and sight-seeing cruises are readily available, as are dock areas for smaller vessels adjacent to the Torpedo Factory Art Center. Personal watercraft are docked at the City marina in downtown Old Town. Potowmack Landing, within the northern boundary of the City, also offers docking and boat ramping as well as sailboat rentals.

Right page: The Alexandria waterfront.

Alexandria

Tourism:
Enjoy Your Visit With Us

Visitors and residents alike enjoy strolling down the brick-laden sidewalks of this old seaport City, taking in the sights and sounds of Alexandria's 300 restaurants and more than 250 antique and specialty shops.

The Alexandria Walking Tour with an 18th century guide is quite a favorite. At Halloween, a Ghosts and Graveyards Walking Tour is available. And the Christmas holidays offer the Scottish Christmas Walk and the Christmas Candlelight Tour, both Alexandria traditions.

Founded by Scottish merchants in 1749 as a seaport, Alexandria has always welcomed visitors by land and by sea. From small European-style hotels to large suite properties, the City offers visitors more than 3,300 sleeping rooms and a wide variety of meeting rooms from which to choose. In all, the hospitality industry in Alexandria consists of 27 hotels and motels. And Alexandria is a popular place to visit. According to the Alexandria Convention and Visitors Association, more than 1.2 million visitors come to the City annually. Those who stay overnight spend $316 million annually, funding 18,045 jobs and 888 travel-related establishments in Alexandria.

Left page: 1. Ramsay House Visitor's Center with passersby. 2. Embassy Suites Hotel, near the King Street Metro Station. ***Right page:*** *1. The elegant Morrison House Hotel. 2. Evening strollers enjoy lower King Street.*

Alexandria

Quaint Retail and Antiques Shops

Perhaps because of its charm as a colonial seaport City, Alexandria is a thriving haven for antiques collectors and aficionados. Along the cobbled streets of the City, 60 antique shops are nestled among the hundreds of historic homes and buildings. No matter what your fancy, collectors of all ages are sure to find treats and deals that match no other in quality and variety.

Art galleries, gift shops and specialty stores carry books, music, jewelry, gourmet food items, Christmas decor, and colorful, ethnic handcrafted and imported products. These businesses are often located near restaurants, historical sites and museums, helping to generate steady foot-traffic and making retail business a strong component of the local economy.

Left, right pages: Many businesses have hung their "shingle," keeping with the traditions of old.

Alexandria

As our first president's hometown, Alexandria holds its renowned George Washington Birthday Celebration Weekend each February, the country's largest of its kind. A parade, a costumed dinner and a 10-K fun run are all part of the annual commemoration. A daily reminder of Washington's contributions to the City and the nation is the George Washington Masonic National Memorial, which sits on Shuter's Hill and dominates the City's skyline. Daily tours are offered and the view of the City in all directions is quite splendid. On a clear day, one can see across the Potomac River into the Maryland countryside.

Old Town Alexandria puts on a magical holiday display beginning the day after Thanksgiving, with twinkling lights leading the way up King Street from the waterfront, west to Shuter's Hill, and along other major streets. The holiday season is capped off with a First Night celebration of the arts on New Year's Eve, fireworks lighting the sky at the George Washington Masonic National Memorial at midnight.

Left page: 1. George Washington National Masonic Memorial on a lovely fall day. 2. Holiday lights give added sparkle to Old Town. *Right page:* 1. George and Martha look-alikes greet the town from their carriage at the annual George Washington Birthday parade. 2. A clown entertains the crowds at the George Washington Birthday parade. 3. The annual Virginia Scottish Games. 4. Bagpipers provide lively music at the George Washington Birthday parade.

Alexandria

There are many other local attractions with ties to Washington and the American Revolution. On North Royal Street at Gadsby's Tavern, George Washington met with fellow patriots regularly and even celebrated his birthday. Nearby at Cameron and North Washington Streets is Christ Church, the first Episcopal church in the City, which counts the first president and Robert E. Lee as parishioners.

On North Fairfax Street is the Carlyle House, home of John Carlyle, one of Alexandria's Scottish founders and earliest wealthy merchants. A meeting was held here to discuss the French and Indian War that led to the drafting of the Stamp Act of 1765. Now restored with period furnishings and operated by the Northern Virginia Regional Park Authority as a museum, this historic property is often rented for weddings and other special events.

Those who consider themselves Civil War buffs come to Alexandria to visit sites such as the Lee-Fendall House on Oronoco Street, home to multiple generations of the Lee family, beginning with Robert E. Lee's aunt and uncle. Across the street is another Lee residence, leased in 1812 by Revolutionary War hero Light-Horse Harry Lee. The house served as the childhood home of Light-Horse Harry's son, Confederate General Robert E. Lee, until the younger Lee's departure for West Point in 1825.

In the West End of Alexandria is the Fort Ward Museum and Park, a former fort used to protect the nation's capital from invasion during the Civil War. The museum sponsors an annual Civil War Union Garrison Day each September, which demonstrates camp life complete with drills, music, a review of the troops and torchlight tours. During the annual George Washington Birthday celebration, the museum also holds Revolutionary War reenactments featuring skirmishes between colonial troops and British Redcoats. Located on West Braddock Road, the Fort Ward Museum and Park is open year-round and features exhibits that document the lives of soldiers.

*Left page: 1. The historic Christ Church. 2. Attendees in period garb at the George Washington Birthday Ball. 3. The parlor of Robert E. Lee's boyhood home. **Right page:** 1. A rear view of the Carlyle House. 2. A colonial battle reenactment at Fort Ward Museum and Park.*

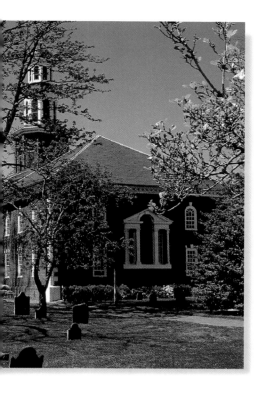

A Diverse
CULTURAL
Fabric

In Alexandria, the arts are a vital, active part of the community. The offerings are remarkably diverse and attract strong government, community and business support. In addition to providing opportunities for participation and personal growth, the arts community in Alexandria serves as an economic stimulus. They run the gamut, from music and theater to visual arts, dance and literature.

Right page: *The arts play a vital role in the appeal of Alexandria.*

Alexandria

The Torpedo Factory Art Center, which alone attracts more than 800,000 visitors a year, is a wonderful enhancement to the artistic offerings of Alexandria. These visitors also fuel the local economy, spending nearly $54.6 million on lodging, food and other purchases while in the City and $2.3 million in the Art Center itself, generating a total of $1.8 million in tax revenue.

At the intersection of King and North Union streets, the Torpedo Factory's mission is three-fold. It functions primarily as an artistic center, where artists in 160 separate studios design, display and sell glass, ceramics, musical instruments, clothing and traditional media. The Torpedo Factory also operates the Art League School, where classes annually provide 8,000 students of all ages with opportunities to learn and experiment with various forms of artistic expression. Finally, the Friends of The Torpedo Factory provide educational programs for city youth, including mentorship programs, in addition to other outreach efforts serving Alexandria schools. Housed in a former World War-era torpedo factory – hence its name – the Torpedo Factory also is the home of the Alexandria Archeology Museum, one of the nation's largest and oldest urban archeology programs.

Left page: 1. The Torpedo Factory Art Center. 2. Weavers are among the diverse artists who occupy the Torpedo Factory. Right page: 1. A Torpedo Factory sculptor explains a piece of work to a customer. 2. A Torpedo Factory artist practices her craft.

Alexandria

Festivals provide another portal into the arts, crafts and cultures of the people who comprise the region. Regular City festivals, held in Market Square, include Armenian, Hispanic American, African American, Scottish, Cypriot, Italian and Irish celebrations. The Scottish Games also draw thousands of attendees each July.

Alexandria celebrates its rich cultural heritage at two museums. The Alexandria Black History Resource Center on North Alfred Street was originally established as a library in 1939 after several young African Americans who were barred from using the City's library staged an early act of civil disobedience. Today, the Black History Resource Center sponsors photography exhibits and displays artifacts such as an 1895 Bible and an 1889 pump organ from the Shiloh Baptist Church. Adjacent to the resource center is the Watson Reading Room, a non-circulating repository whose works feature African American culture and history.

The second museum is the Lyceum on South Washington Street. Operated by the City's Office of Historic Alexandria, the Lyceum preserves the comprehensive history of Alexandria and the surrounding Northern Virginia area, from 1749 to the present. Its handsome Greek Revival building was constructed in 1839 and served as hospital during the Civil War. Following post-war use as a home and then offices, the Lyceum was saved from demolition by local preservationists and the City of Alexandria in the 1970s and opened in 1974 as Alexandria's bicentennial visitors center.

Diverse nationalities, including the Hispanic, Latino and Asian communities, make the city a balanced and friendly place to live, work and visit. Alexandria is also a community of many faiths. Some places of worship such as Christ Church date back to the 18th century and add to the City's heritage.

Left page: 1. Market Square is the site of the Polish Festival. 2. The Refugee Festival. **Right page:** *1. The African American Festival. 2. The Native American Festival. 3. The Lyceum, Alexandria's history museum.*

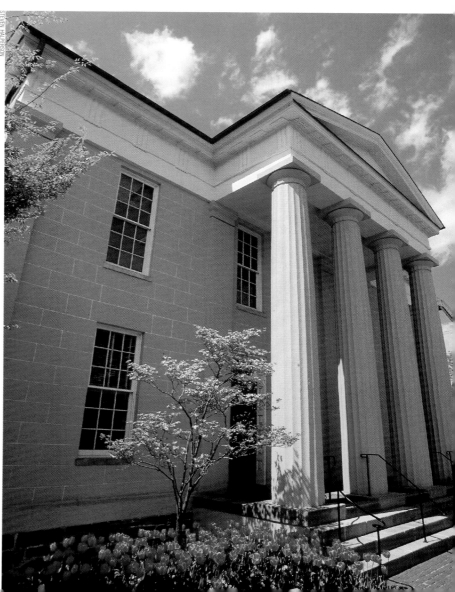

Alexandria

A Bevy of Natural Resources

Alexandria has more than 900 acres of public parks and open spaces, and children, adults and pets all enjoy the beauty of these natural sanctuaries. The City also has a rich array of recreational facilities. Residents of all ages enjoy the many concerts and special activities offered by the Alexandria Department of Recreation, Parks and Cultural Activities. Tennis lessons, swimming, basketball, day trips for senior citizens and arts and crafts classes are but a few of the programs offered by the City and area community organizations.

The wave slide and wave pool at Cameron Run Regional Park on Eisenhower Avenue is a wonderful place to spend a muggy summer afternoon. The park also offers miniature golf for duffers, young and old. In the West End is the Ramsey Nature Center and Dora Kelly Nature Park. There's no telling what natural wonders will be discovered on a nature walk or through the center's many interpretive programs featuring the plants, animals, geology and archeology of the region.

Left page: 1. A parrot entertains tourists on a pier in Old Town. 2. Sailboats at Washington Sailing Marina. 3. George Washington Middle School Choir performs at Market Square. *Right page:* 1. Children on a nature walk at Ramsay Nature Center. 2. The water troughs at Cameron Run Regional Park provide hours of fun. 3. Children swimming at the Dora Kelley Nature Park. 4. A guided walk through a creek is a great way to cool off.

Alexandria

The trail along George Washington Memorial Parkway is another majestic experience for those who enjoy the great outdoors. The 18-mile path meanders along the Potomac River, ending south of the City at Mount Vernon, and it is especially popular with area cyclists, runners, walkers and rollerbladers. Those who frequent the trail in the early morning hours can often look out upon the daily training routine of Alexandria's T.C. Williams High School crew team, each member rhythmically rowing in the soft breeze.

The GW path passes by Jones Point Park, where a refurbished lighthouse stands on the banks of the Potomac River at the southernmost point of Alexandria. It is at this park each July that the City holds its annual birthday and Independence Day celebration, replete with cake, music and, of course, fireworks.

*Left page: 1. A biker enjoys the natural beauty of the trail along the George Washington Parkway. 2. Children biking along the waterfront. **Right page:** 1. Crew team at sunrise. 2. The Jones Point Light house. 3. A fire-eater entertains Time-Life employees at their annual picnic. 4. Waterfront Festival fireworks cascade across the sky at Oronoco Bay Park.*

A Community of Friendly
NEIGHBORS

Old Town is perhaps the best-known neighborhood in Alexandria. On the eastern edge of the City and next to the Potomac River, Old Town residents live in a tasteful mix of townhomes and apartments. The historical flavor of the City is pervasive, as many homes are registered with the City's Historic Alexandria Foundation. The Federal, Georgian and Greek Revival-style buildings amidst updated contemporary architecture provide a comprehensive look at the past and the future of this historic City.

Right page: *A quaint Old Town street, one of Alexandria's many scenic benefits.*

Alexandria

Central to the neighborhood on Saturday mornings in Old Town is the Farmer's Market, held weekly in Market Square since 1749. Produce, homemade baked goods, flowers and crafts are part of the offerings of this Alexandria institution, which is quite a draw for both Alexandrians and visitors near and far.

Del Ray, to the northwest of Old Town, has been added to the National Historic Register for the classic architecture found in many of its houses and commercial buildings. An eclectic area known for its Soho-like charisma, this neighborhood community is a maturing economic center with many small and large businesses.

The community has stately Victorian and World War-era homes interspersed with new townhomes and single family dwellings. Young at heart and in its median age, Del Ray is home to both young families with children and older residents who have lived for many years in the community that is bounded by Route 1 on the east and Russell Road on the west. Runners and walkers enjoy the lovely tree-lined streets and its many green parks.

Left page: 1. Old Town North. 2. Architectural detail of Prince Street. Right page: 1. Children enjoy the Mount Vernon Avenue Block Party. 2. A home in Alexandria's Del Ray neighborhood. 3. Fruit and vegetables are popular offerings at the Farmer's Market each Saturday.

Alexandria

The West End of Alexandria is rapidly developing. Townhomes, condominiums and apartments are interspersed with professional offices, retail shops and restaurants. Rolling hills and winding streets dressed with flowering bushes and tall trees make the neighborhoods of the West End wonderful places for families with children as well as young professionals and grandparents who want good quality of life on a daily basis.

Rosemont, the community north of the George Washington Masonic National Memorial, is an older neighborhood noted for its many Sears Catalog residences. These ready-made kit homes were purchased from Sears Roebuck in the early part of the 1900's and constructed upon delivery. Amid stuccoed bungalows and brick townhomes, Rosemont has big, old oak trees astride wide streets with plenty of room for bicyclists, runners and walkers. (Plus, as neighborhood children will attest, Shuter's Hill is a great place for winter-time sledding!)

Rosemont's convenience is an added plus for many residents, as they like the feel of being just outside Old Town and near to the King Street Metro station.

*Left page: 1. The Landmark area of Alexandria, also called the West End. 2. A high-rise apartment building in the West End. **Right page:** 1. The Rosemont neighborhood near Old Town. 2. An apartment community. 3. Sledding on Shuter's Hill, near Rosemont.*

Alexandria

Seminary Valley is a beautiful enclave, known for its stately homes. Nestled between the West End and Old Town on the east, Seminary Valley is the site of many newer, larger homes. On summer evenings you can smell the scent of barbecued chicken and hear the muffled cries of delight as children race under sprinklers as a humid day comes to a soft close.

Nearby is another well-established Alexandria neighborhood–Beverley Hills. Tucked in the northwest corner of the City, this neighborhood hosts sizable brick homes with expansive green lawns. Young and old Alexandrians enjoy biking and walking through the canopy of leaves offered by the community's towering trees in both summer and fall.

Arlandria, to the north of Old Town and bounded on the south by Del Ray, is the site of exciting change and growth. Condominiums, apartments and appealing single-family homes dot this vibrant community where children play basketball at the Cora Kelly Recreation Center and locals drop by the Waffle Shop for coffee on weekday mornings.

Carlyle Towers is the latest addition to the blossoming Eisenhower corridor. Ultimately a 600-unit, three-building condominium, it is the first of many residential developments being built in this new neighborhood. South of Duke Street and the King Street Metro station, the freshly paved streets and newly planted flowers of Carlyle lend beautiful prescience to what the corridor one day will become.

Left page: 1. A home in Seminary Valley. 2. Beverley Hills.
Right page: Carlyle Towers, one of Alexandria' newer condominium communities. 2. Arlandria's Waffle Shop.

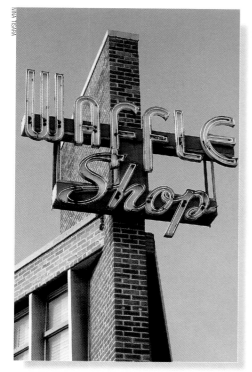

A Resourceful
CITY

The City of Alexandria offers a high quality of life for its people and its businesses. Operating under a city manager structure, the Alexandria City government is highly regarded for its consistent record of responsible management. A city council of six elected members and a mayor provide policy guidance to the city manager, who is responsible for the day-to-day operations of the government. More than 100 boards, commissions and task forces, comprised of representatives from the business and residential communities, offer their expertise and input to the city council and city manager for use in the conduct of their duties.

The City's AAA bond rating places it among only 17 cities and 14 counties in the United States with a similar rating by both of Wall Street's rating agencies, Standard and Poor's and Moody's Investors Service. A major draw for both businesses and residents, Alexandria offers favorable real estate and property tax rates, in comparison to neighboring jurisdictions.

Right page: An ice cream social at the Friendship Firehouse.

Alexandria

The Alexandria City Public Schools provide a quality educational environment for the City's youth. From its Technology Initiative to its above-average expenditure per pupil, Alexandria schools offer students the skills they need to succeed as adults in a diverse world that is constantly growing and changing. The school system has a well-regarded gifted and talented program, and its advanced placement and honors courses are filled with youth who provide special promise for tomorrow's advancements and achievements.

Many young children spend afternoons and evenings at the Alexandria City Public Library. In fact, the recently refurbished Kate Waller Barrett branch on Queen Street in Old Town is a favorite place for story hour. Senior citizens, high school and college students alike also appreciate access to books, tapes and multimedia resources.

Left page: 1. Alexandria school children using markers to express themselves artistically. 2. Students at work on a biology project at T.C. Williams High School. **Right page:** *1. Story hour at one of Alexandria's many libraries. 2. Graduation day at T.C. Williams High School.*

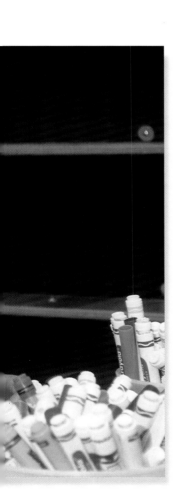

Alexandria

The Alexandria City Police Department works closely with City residents and businesses to ensure a safe environment for everyone. Its successful community policing program enhances the department's continuing efforts to make Alexandria a pleasant community. The Alexandria City Fire Department also conducts public safety programs, such as its noted School Fire Safety Program for youth at public and private elementary schools in the City.

Public access to affordable health care is a priority for Alexandrians. The city has an excellent health care infrastructure with the Casey Clinic, the City Health Department and its Emergency Medical System. Inova's Alexandria Hospital on Seminary Road and Mount Vernon Hospital just south of the city, have long histories of providing excellent care. There is also Lynn House, a Christian Science hospital located on West Braddock Road. A strong network of primary care physicians can respond to practically any health care need of area residents. The metropolitan region is also served by a number of medical schools and federal health research facilities, which serve as tremendous resources for area health professionals.

In addition, City residents have quick, affordable access to the entire metropolitan area through its many transportation venues. Alexandria's DASH bus system, Metrorail Metrobus service, in addition to Virginia Railway Express and AMTRAK service via Alexandria's recently refurbished Union Station, offer commuting options for those who work in Alexandria or are just visiting.

Left page: 1. Police talking with children at the St. Patrick's Day parade. 2. The train at the King Street Metro Station.
Right page: Community policing is an important part of the Alexandria Police Department's outreach efforts.

Looking Ahead to the 21st Century

Exciting years lie ahead for the City of Alexandria and its residential and business communities.

New growth in technology and an expanding tax base make the City an attractive option for

employers and employees. Planned improvements to infrastructure will be complete, and

today's new business communities will be fully developed. Amidst the charm of the old seaport

City, Alexandria organizations of all kinds and sizes are poised to thrive as the region becomes

even more of an economic powerhouse.

CORPORATE PROFILES IN EXCELLENCE

Alexandria Chamber of Commerce

The Alexandria Chamber of Commerce is a non-profit organization of more than 1,000 businesses dedicated to promoting a strong economic climate and high quality of life in the City of Alexandria. The Chamber offers a variety of programs and services to assist member firms in promoting and expanding their businesses. Through aggressive lobbying efforts, the Alexandria Chamber represents member interests on state and federal issues important to businesses in Alexandria.

The Chamber's 29-member Board of Directors, 15 committees and task forces and nine staff members develop an Annual Program of Action to plan for future improvements, including technological advancements and special programs to assist local businesses' economic success. Details of these goals can be obtained by visiting the Chamber's website at www.alexander.com.

As **the** voice of business in Alexandria, the Chamber deliberates legislative, tax, transportation and land use issues that impact the local business community. The Chamber has played a leadership role in recent years in lobbying to keep Alexandria's tax rates among the lowest in Northern Virginia, promoting public parking opportunities in the City's historic district, and generating business support for the local welfare reform effort.

The organization's ability to build business and community support for various initiatives, provides long-term economic benefits to the City. Marketing business opportunities in Alexandria is important, and the Chamber is a key partner in the effort to expand the City's employment base.

For example, the Chamber works closely with the Small Business Development Center at the George Washington University Alexandria Graduate Education Center to help counsel and guide emerging businesses. In addition, the Alexandria Chamber has a close working relationship with the Alexandria Economic Development

Partnership, the Alexandria Convention and Visitors Association and other organizations to market Alexandria as a dynamic shopping, dining, business and tourist destination.

Among its many programs, the Chamber cosponsors Alexandria Technology Achievement Week, which recognizes technology firms as a prominent component of the Alexandria business community. It also is coordinating a new Technology Council, striving to integrate Alexandria's 164 technology firms into the local business community. In recent years, the Chamber partnered with the City of Alexandria and the Alexandria Branch of the NAACP to develop recommendations on improving communications and services to small and minority businesses. As a result, a Small and Minority Business Fair and fi-

nancing forum were jointly sponsored by the Chamber, the City, and the NAACP to promote the wide variety of firms in Alexandria.

Networking opportunities abound at the Chamber, with monthly programs drawing hundreds of business

people to the morning and evening programs. Management seminars provide members with effective business practices. The Chamber's **Who's Who** membership directory, distributed to 2,000 businesses, and its **Business Guide**, distributed to 20,000 households and businesses in the City, are popular publications.

Member businesses are promoted by the Alexandria Chamber of Commerce through thousands of phone, fax, correspondence and website requests. Referrals are made only to Chamber members, a free membership service. The Alexandria Chamber is the third largest and one of the most effective Chambers in the Washington, D.C. region. Call 703-549-1000 for more information.

Alexandria Economic Development Partnership, Inc.

ALEXANDRIA
A Unique Place To Do Business

In a joint effort, City officials, business owners and residents work together to strengthen the local economy of Alexandria.

This effort has formed the dynamics of the business community to increase its presence in Alexandria.

The Alexandria Economic Development Partnership, Inc. is the link of this joint effort implementing many of the recommendations with significant results.

Whether you are planning to expand or to locate your business in Alexandria, the Alexandria Economic Development Partnership, Inc. stands ready to forward your progress.
Discover what we already know.

Alexandria Economic
Development Partnership, Inc.
99 Canal Center Plaza
Suite 4, River Level
Alexandria, VA 22314
703-739-3820
Fax: 703-739-1384
e-mail: alexecon@erols.com

Alexandria –
building on its past and poised for its future.

Photo by Ellen Callaway

Business, Finance, and Professions

Potomac Partners, Inc.

Potomac Partners Inc. is a commercial real estate development and hotel management firm headquartered in Alexandria. Founded in 1993, it offers management and advisory services for the acquisition, development, operation and sale of suburban office, flex and industrial properties, as well as limited and full-service hotels.

Potomac Partners places special emphasis on hotel acquisition and development, ranging from limited service hotels to first class full-service conference facilities. With more than 700 employees, the company presently operates seven hotels for a combined inventory of almost 1,300 guest rooms. In Alexandria, these proper-

ties include the Holiday Inn Hotel & Suites, the Ramada Plaza Hotel and the Old Colony Inn.

The company also operates a number of commercial projects in the metropolitan Washington area. Its commercial office buildings in Alexandria include the Parkway Building, a 100,000 square-foot office building on the George Washington Parkway south of National Airport in Alexandria and North Point, a 68,750 square-foot flex office project in the shadow of the Braddock Road Metro Station.

Within reach of Alexandria's historic district and less than five miles from Washington, D.C., the Parkway Building is close to both the ambiance of Old Town and the seat of the Fed-

eral Government. The building is also accessible to public transportation, with Metro bus service and the Braddock Road Metro Station less than two minutes away.

The building's appeal in part relies on the richly treed environment of the adjacent parkway. Designed with an abundance of windows and multiple windowed corner offices, the building's L-shape offers flexible floor planning. A lovely paneled lobby greets you upon arrival, and solar insulated windows and a climate control system with separate wing and individual perimeter zones ensure personal comfort and minimum tenant energy costs. In addition, the fully secured building has almost an acre of

underground parking for the convenience and safety of its tenants. Its largest tenant is Harris Corporation, a Fortune 200 technology company.

North Point offers flex office, industrial and retail space a block from Metro with high visibility on U.S. Route 1 and close proximity to both National Airport and the Beltway. With eleven bays from 4,750 to 9,750 square feet in size, the project easily accommodates a wide range of tenants, growing technology companies as well as retail uses. Zoned for high density mixed use, this site also represents a significant development opportunity at a Metro location.

Ramada Plaza Hotel & Conference Center

Whether in Washington for business or for pleasure, consider staying at the Ramada Plaza Hotel & Conference Center. Midway between the White House and Mount Vernon, the Ramada Plaza offers easy access to the area's many historic sites.

Travelers will enjoy the hospitality and dedicated service of the Ramada Plaza Hotel. Due to the staff's outstanding attention to service, style and

ambiance, the hotel has been named a top performing Ramada Plaza for each of the last ten years.

A majority of the hotel's 258 guest rooms have picturesque views of the Potomac River, Nation's Capital and/or Historic Old Town. Smoking and non-smoking floors are available.

Chequers, the Ramada's restaurant and lounge, offers breakfast and lunch

buffets, nightly dinner specials and a Sunday brunch buffet. Room service is also available daily.

Looking for a place to unwind? The lounge, complete with comfortable couches and chairs, is the ideal place to meet informally with friends, family or colleagues. Or, for a comfortable place to relax in the morning, join fellow guests and the Ramada Plaza executive staff for complimen-

tary coffee in the lobby.

Meeting space is plentiful. The Ramada Plaza's Executive Board Room, which seats 20 and is complete with built-in audio visual equipment, is a popular place for board meetings and other senior-level meetings. In all, the Ramada Plaza has eight meeting rooms, including the Grand Ballroom with flexibility for smaller breakout meetings, which can accommodate from 10 to 650 people.

Modem-compatible telephones with voice mail are provided in each guest room, as are coffee makers, hair dryers, irons and ironing boards. Guests can enjoy the nearby fitness center and tennis courts, as well as the 18-mile jogging path adjacent to the hotel which follows the Potomac River from the Lincoln Memorial to Mount Vernon Plantation (the home of George Washington). Visit the Ramada Plaza's rooftop pool, open from Memorial Day to Labor Day.

Ample complimentary parking is provided. Courtesy shuttle service is offered to and from National Airport, National Airport Metrorail Station and

Old Town Alexandria. A variety of area restaurants are within walking distance of the hotel, or within a short 15-minute drive into Washington, D.C.

Holiday Inn Hotel & Suites

The Holiday Inn Hotel & Suites in Alexandria's famed Historic District adjoins the cobblestone streets and the charm of Old Town. Whether long- or short-term, the Holiday Inn offers travelers a variety of amenities that can make travel much easier and more enjoyable.

Conveniently located on the doorstep of our nation's capital, the hotel's complimentary shuttle provides transportation to and from National Airport and Metrorail Station, both just two miles away. Guests can park for free in the hotel's spacious garage.

Each room is equipped with comforts that are designed to make business travel as comfortable and productive as possible. Guest rooms have automated voice mail and data ports for quick laptop connections, in addition to individual coffee makers, irons and hair dryers.

The Holiday Inn's 178 oversized guest rooms include 17 spacious suites, complete with refrigerators, dinner service for six, microwave ovens and a wet bar. Six of the larger suites are equipped with whirlpool tubs and are perfect for senior executives who are house hunting or in need of space to meet or entertain while in town.

Visit the hotel's full-scale Fitness Center, complete with heated indoor/outdoor pool, saunas and extensive exercise equipment. Traditions Restaurant and Lounge, located on the ground level, features American menu favorites for lunch and dinner as well as evening entertainment and Sunday brunch. A grocery store across the street makes shopping convenient.

The Holiday Inn Hotel & Suites is an excellent choice for small and large meetings and conferences. The hotel can accommodate your organization's every need in its Commonwealth Ballroom or one of

seven other meeting rooms, equipped to handle 10 to 750 guests for meetings, exhibits and social gatherings. Plus, the hotel's beautiful Garden Gazebo provides the perfect setting for evening receptions and other special social occasions.

A business center in the hotel lobby offers copying, faxing, word processing services and computer and equipment rental, in addition to many other office services. Conference and meeting support services, including audio visual equipment and services, also are available.

Within walking distance of Old Town's many ethnic restaurants and quaint shops, the Holiday Inn Hotel & Suites is the perfect place to do business in Old Town Alexandria.

Best Western Old Colony Inn

Set on three and a half beautifully landscaped acres in Old Town Alexandria, the Best Western Old Colony Inn is ideally located for exploring the many attractions that the Capital region has to offer. Browse the quaint shops and charming boutiques, cruise the Potomac by river boat or savor the cuisine of Alexandria's fine restaurants.

The White House, Capital Hill and Washington, D.C.'s many monuments and museums are just minutes away,

conveniently accessible by Metrorail. The hotel provides complimentary shuttle service to and from Washington National Airport and the airport Metrorail stop, just two miles away. Free on-site parking is also offered. Whatever your adventure, the Best Western Old Colony Inn offers a welcome retreat at day's end.

The buildings and grounds at the Best Western Old Colony Inn are designed to reflect the sense of history and gracious style that makes Old Town so inviting. The hotel offers 151 nicely appointed guest rooms. Begin the day with complimentary continental breakfast and coffee in the lobby.

Amid full days of sightseeing or business, relax and unwind in the Fitness Center adjacent to the hotel, offering a complete exercise room with indoor and outdoor pools, whirlpool and saunas. For total relaxation, indulge in the lovely atmosphere, fine cuisine and attentive service at Tradition's Restaurant next door. A complete room service menu is also available for in-room dining.

The Best Western Old Colony Inn's Conference Center, with more than 2,500 square feet of flexible meeting space, provides a unique setting for business and social functions or private retreats. A business center is adjacent to the hotel, offering complete office support services and equipment, in addition to full audio visual and conference support services.

Of special note, the hotel has been recognized by Best Western International for its outstanding quality of service. Come and experience the award-winning environment that has people returning to visit us year after year.

Whether your final destination is in the Washington area or another locale, we hope that you will experience the elegant charm of the Best Western Old Colony Inn.

ABAN Computers

An integrator of microcomputer-based systems and enterprise networks since 1989, ABAN Computers focuses on high-end advanced communications solutions for its clients. It provides consulting, maintenance, design and implementation, technical support, outsourcing and training for PC-based enterprise environments. Of particular note, ABAN specializes in cross-platform connectivity in Local and Wide Area Networks.

Based in Alexandria, ABAN Computers serves the entire Washington metropolitan area. In recent years, the company has expanded into the international arena. ABAN has been a member of numerous trade missions led by the United States Department of Commerce, and as a result, has forged alliances with existing computer systems integrators in Sri Lanka, Panama, Bolivia, Kazakstan, Poland, Ghana and Burkina Faso.

The company's success can be attributed to its strong commitment to total customer satisfaction. According to Amir Sohrabi, ABAN vice president, "our philosophy can be summarized in three words: quality, dependability and expertise." By maintaining the best technology with the highest quality of systems consultations, service and support, ABAN is able to anticipate both technological advances and advise its clients accordingly how to plan for such market fluctuations. It is this trait that makes ABAN's services especially valuable.

ABAN's team of expert technicians and advisors are certified and prepared to provide each client with ready, cost-effective solutions that increase an organization's competitive advantage. For example, as Lotus, Microsoft and Novell partners, ABAN provides sales and support for products such as Lotus Notes, Microsoft Applications and Back Office products, and Novell Intranet and Groupwise products. In short, ABAN Computers' application software design and development services reflect and accommodate customers' current needs while still maintaining the flexibility to change or upgrade a computer systems' capabilities.

The company has strong relationships with more than 150 premiere hardware manufacturers and distributors that provide microcomputers, printers and communication equipment, including IBM, Hewlett

Packard, Compaq, 3Com and AST, among others. All equipment proposed and supported are compatible in nature, and non-proprietary to ensure that its customers are not locked into a "sole-source" line of response and support. Each client requirement is evaluated on an individual basis and options proposed are ones that ABAN specialists feel best fit the particular situation or need.

ABAN's consulting service team designs and implements enterprise-wide solutions that fit specific business models by focusing on the integration of heterogeneous networks that serve as the platform for today's application. The company's extensive "needs analysis" determines the best technology needed by an organization and proposes scalable solutions that can effectively address any business situation.

Once the ideal hardware and software have been identified, ABAN's technical teams pre-configure all hardware, pre-load all software and pre-test all equipment. The firm's field technicians and systems engineers deliver the equipment to your locations, establish all connections, verify operability, conduct end-user orientation and perform final integration or configuration required. Installation can also be arranged after work hours to minimize interruptions.

Whether connecting workstations in one or several locations, locally or even globally, ABAN's technical team can assist with creating and implementing optimal networking capabilities. The company's services include everything from network design to implementation and testing.

ABAN offers a wide range of flexible and affordable service plans to help protect an organization's investments and keep it fully operational. Maintenance can be performed at the office, scheduled when convenient. On-site emergency service is available 24 hours a day, seven days a week.

ABAN also carriers a complete line of the latest products, from accessories and cables to desktops and interface cards, from modems and scanners to servers and hubs. It is for this reason that ABAN clients have come to rely on the company as a reliable supplier of technological solutions at reasonable costs.

With a full staff of highly qualified and trained experts, ABAN is truly equipped with the latest computer technology and tools. The firm assists its clients in three ways – either on-site, through a remote diagnostic test or by phone. From system design and planning to integration, installation, maintenance and upgrades, the ABAN technical team possesses the knowl-

edge and expertise that keeps a system running smoothly.

ABAN also provides training. The firm teams with professional training providers across the country so that its customers have access to the latest in new technology. These training courses are developed by professional industry trainers and are designed for anyone involved in using, installing, administering, configuring and troubleshooting software and hardware.

To put ABAN Computers' technical prowess and expertise to work for your organization, contact them at 703-739-8833.

STEVEN HALPERSON

Hoffman Management

Known as a visionary and leader in the development community for more than 40 years, the legacy of Hubert N. Hoffman began in 1958 when he used his life savings to purchase 70 acres of destitute swamp land surrounded by three junk yards and a run-down trailer park, in what is now known as Alexandria's Eisenhower Valley. Hoffman is known as the "Father of the Eisenhower Valley."

Friends assured him his investment was foolish and that he would lose everything. Even Alexandria's director of public works was skeptical when Hoffman told him he intended to construct high-rise office buildings on the site and "to make that swamp a paradise."

Hoffman then searched for six years for a lender with the foresight to provide the financing for a hotel on his Eisenhower Valley property. Finally, in 1966, Hoffman completed construction of the Eisenhower Avenue Holiday Inn, long a landmark in the Valley. Across the street from the Hoffman Center, the hotel has spacious meeting rooms, attractively appointed and comfortable guest rooms and a wonderful full-service restaurant on the premises.

He then focused on fulfilling his vow to build high-rise office buildings on the site. After winning a U.S. General Services Administration bid by a mere four cents, Hoffman began constructing a 336,000 square-foot structure known as Hoffman Building I,

which was completed in 1968. Hoffman's dream continued with the completion of the 750,000 square-foot Hoffman Building II in 1972.

Hoffman delights in telling listeners the now-legendary tale of how the Valley obtained its name. Shortly after acquiring the land for the Hoffman Center, Hoffman was undecided about what to call this new area of the city. Traveling on the Capital Beltway, a car passed him with an "Eisenhower for President" bumper sticker. Hence the name of Eisenhower Valley was born.

Always involved in every aspect of the leasing and management of the buildings, Hoffman still visits his on-site office daily and gives personal attention to each and every detail. This "personal touch" is highly regarded in the development community and is well-known among his tenants. A family business in the truest sense, Hoffman and his dedicated staff have an impressive record of responding to tenant questions or concerns with the utmost in professional attention and response with dispatch. It is for this reason that praise for Hoffman's management style and flair for the beautification of his lovely campus-like grounds abound.

His generosity and fervor for fitness are well-known. As one of the first to perceive the importance of exercise to personal and professional well-being, he added a health facility to the property in 1986 for the benefit of tenants as well as Hoffman employees. He recently enhanced the facility with the donation of more than $20,000 of equipment for the benefit of his tenants, which represent a mix of public and private organizations.

Hoffman also had the vision to donate a portion of his land to the City of Alexandria in 1978 for the construction of the neighboring Eisenhower Metro rail station, located across the street. The sta-

tion provides Hoffman Center and other Valley residents with convenient and rapid access to the entire metropolitan area, including Old Town Alexandria, National Airport, Crystal City, the Pentagon, Rosslyn, downtown D.C., Capitol Hill and suburban Maryland.

At the junction of the Capital Beltway (I-495) and Telegraph Road, the Hoffman Center is also served by Metro bus, Alexandria's DASH bus service, and the Fairfax County Connector bus service. Hoffman Center is a quick, seven-minute walk to Alexandria's Union Station, where AMTRAK provides access to major business centers on the entire eastern seaboard as well as other U.S. and Canadian cities. Train service via the Virginia Railway Express is also available at Union Station, which connects the

Eisenhower Valley with outlying jurisdictions such as Fredericksburg and Manassas.

Hoffman Center tenants also enjoy close proximity to Old Town. Tenants often spend their lunch or evening hours shopping at the fine boutiques in Alexandria, just a ten-minute walk or one Metro stop away. And many have found lunch or dinnertime dining "al fresco" at nearby restaurants and cafes to be a most enjoyable way to experience the area's historic charm. Hoffman Center residents truly are in the center of it all.

A legend in the Northern Virginia development community, the Swamp Fox, as Hoffman is affectionately known, possessed the leadership and strength of character necessary to make his dream come true.

Today, hundreds of other organizations have joined with Hoffman to make the Eisenhower Valley a stronghold of public and private organizations. It is in large part because of Hoffman's tremendous foresight and his ability to convince others of his plans that the Valley has become such a flourishing success.

Washington Gas

Headquartered in Washington, D.C., Washington Gas provides natural gas and other consumer services to more than 795,000 residential, commercial and industrial customers throughout the Washington metropolitan area.

For more than 150 years, Washington Gas has been improving the quality of life in the nation's capital. In the early 1800s, residents constantly complained about its muddy, unlit streets and used candles or oil for illumination.

Following Washington's first successful use of gas lighting in the Treasury Building in 1841, natural gas was used to light several hotels and buildings at George Town College. The growing popularity of natural gas lighting in Baltimore and Philadelphia also helped spur Congressional approval for the incorporation of Washington Gas Light Company in 1848. The result was the first natural gas company in the United States chartered by Congress. By the end of the year the company had gas mains laid, lamp posts and lanterns erected, and had lit the president's house.

The company survived the Civil War with a little help from President Abraham Lincoln. Despite a severe coal shortage and transportation problems at the time, President Lincoln wrote a letter to the president of the Baltimore and Ohio Railroad to explain the importance of transporting coal to Washington Gas to avert a gas crisis in the nation's capital. The request brought coal to the city, allowing the capital's homes and streets to remain lit as the war raged on.

As the 20th century dawned, Washington Gas continued growing. It expanded into Maryland and Virginia. The company weathered the fuel shortages of two world wars and the constant changes associated with consistent, sometimes rapid, growth. The company has paid dividends to shareholders for 145 consecutive years, which is one of the longest dividend records for companies listed on the New York Stock Exchange.

Deregulation of the energy industry has ushered in the latest round of change for Washington Gas. In response to the transformation of the industry, the company is redefining its mission and reprioritizing its goals. There is a renewed commitment to customers, which is evident in the company's mission statement: "We will be the customer's choice for energy, profitably offering all products and services at competitive prices."

Today natural gas is the fuel of choice for more than 9 out of 10 new home buyers in the Washington metropolitan area. As the company advances, so does its community spirit. Washington Gas and its 2,000 employees continue a long tradition of reinvesting in the communities it serves. In fact, Washington Gas was named 1995 Business of the Year by the District of Columbia Chamber of Commerce in recognition of its good business practices and community involvement.

In 1983, the company organized the Washington Area Fuel Fund (WAFF) to provide a vehicle for the private sector to supplement government funding for energy assistance. The Salvation Army administers the program, and Washington Gas pays all administrative costs so that every penny donated to WAFF goes to help

people in need. Since the program began, nearly $9 million has been disbursed to assist people in more than 30,000 cases.

Washington Gas is a strong advocate of education, providing materials, scholarships and funding to area institutions. The company participates in the Christmas in April project, which refurbishes homes for the elderly, persons who are disabled and low-in-

come families. These are just a few of the company's activities that help enhance the quality of life for those living in the Washington metropolitan area.

With a strong foundation of innovative marketing, sharpened customer focus and five years of record-setting earnings, Washington Gas is poised to excel in the new era of competitive energy services. The company is testing new markets and exploring and developing new products and services. Customer choice is critical, and Washington Gas is focusing on serving all of its customers' energy needs. The company plans to apply its gas marketing and distribution know-how to the sale of electricity as soon as laws and regulations are modified to permit such sales.

Washington Gas is looking forward to its industry's continued evolution and stands ready to take advantage of the opportunities offered by the rapid change. For more information about Washington Gas, visit the company's Website at http://www.washgas.com.

Commonwealth Atlantic Properties Inc.

Commonwealth Atlantic Properties Inc. is the owner and developer of Potomac Yard, a 300-acre mixed-use community of retail businesses, offices and homes at the northern edge of Old Town Alexandria.

Formerly the RF&P Corporation, Commonwealth Atlantic was purchased in 1996 by an investment fund managed by the Lazard Freres Real Estate Investors, LLC. The company owns and manages a portfolio of commercial properties located along the Alexandria-Richmond corridor.

Potomac Yard Center, the Yard's highly successful retail center, is located on Route 1 one-half mile south of National Airport. It includes prominent national and regional retailers selling men and women's clothing, pet supplies, furnishings, sporting gear and books. Alexandrians are especially appreciative of the Yard's 76,000 square-foot grocery store, one of the region's largest.

A 16-screen movie complex at the rear of Potomac Yard Center makes it

an attractive evening and weekend destination. The center's many restaurants have quickly become popular gathering places for breakfast, lunch and dinner — or even a post-movie snack.

Designed as more than a place to shop and dine, more than 3.75 million square feet of top-quality office space is planned for the Yard. Two hotels totaling 625 rooms will provide first-class accommodations for both business travelers and tourists.

Commonwealth Atlantic has made substantial improvements to the infrastructure and roadways adjacent to Potomac Yard to promote the safe and smooth flow of traffic in the vicinity. A boon for residents and commuters to the Yard, construction

of a new Metro station is also being planned.

The southernmost end of Potomac Yard will house an array of townhomes and mid-rise condominiums and apartments. Near both George Washington Memorial Parkway and Route 1, these 2,000 mid-priced to upscale homes will offer ready accessibility to the area's major transportation hubs and National Airport.

Taking into account the natural beauty of the area, Commonwealth Atlantic carefully planned Potomac Yard so that it includes a system of landscaped parklands and bike and running trails. The open space area near Slater's Lane is used quite often by neighborhood youth for outdoor recreational activities.

Potomac Yard represents a well-planned mix of retail, restaurant, office and residential developments. For more information about Commonwealth Atlantic and its many other successful property developments, call 703-838-5680.

Eakin/Youngentob Associates

Eakin/Youngentob Associates is a development team focused on creating high quality, lifestyle friendly communities in premium locations near downtown Washington, D.C. With over 30 years' development experience, Terry Eakin and Bob Youngentob formed Eakin/Youngentob Associates with a commitment to delivering the highest level of customer satisfaction and professionalism every step of the way.

Since its inception, Eakin/Youngentob Associates has been recognized for excellence by having won more industry awards than any other Washington area builder. In 1995 Eakin/Youngentob won the coveted Judge's Choice Award, which represents the most distinguished Finest for Family Living Award in the Washington metropolitan region. Eakin/Youngentob is proud of having

won the prestigious 1996 Entrepreneur of the Year Award for the real estate industry.

Alexandria's Ford's Landing and Old Town Village are the company's newest communities in a list that includes some of the most desirable addresses in the Washington area. Ford's Landing is just steps from the beautiful Potomac River and Old Town Alexandria's historic sites, charming shops and renowned restaurants. The new riverfront townhomes at Ford's Landing offer old world charm and modern comfort. With architecture reflecting the very history of Alexandria, homeowners can choose from Colonial, Victorian and Georgian designs. These gracious, stately homes boast spacious interiors with hardwood floors, marble foyers and high ceilings, and the finest craftsmanship

in the smallest details, like brass bathroom fixtures and marbleized tile.

Old Town Village blends traditional charm with best in city convenience and neighborhood amenities. A short walk to the Metro and the nearby shops and restaurants of Old Town, it offers the additional benefits of a community club with year-round exercise room and indoor spa, a private outdoor pool and off-street parking. The homes of Old Town Village include garage townhomes and courtyard homes with Colonial architecture, both with luxury appointments. A first floor master suite, offered in the courtyard homes, is a rare find in a new home today.

Please call us at 703-525-5565 for more information about making Old Town Village or Ford's Landing your new residence.

Holland Engineering

Since its founding in 1939, Holland Engineering has provided services in the areas of civil engineering, land surveying and land planning.

Holland's expertise covers all phases of project development. From complete surveying functions that include field operations, subdivision design, platting and mapping, to land planning for site analysis and project feasibility, the firm has a strong track record of service to numerous public and private organizations located in the Washington metropolitan area. A testament to its diverse capabilities, the firm has completed a broad array of residential, commercial, industrial and institutional projects.

Holland's impressive portfolio reflects a large number of Northern Virginia area projects in particular. From the Alexandria Redevelopment Housing Authority to Habitat For Humanity, from the Alexandria Yacht Basin to mixed use development in the Eisenhower Valley, Holland has served a wide range of civil engineering needs.

Holland professionals are also skilled in conceptual or preliminary engineering design, including the definition of a project or program scope, as well as final engineering design and specification for streets, sewers and utility lines.

Finally, the firm's team of dedicated professionals have also defined specifications for comprehensive storm water management and for landscaping purposes. The company is highly regarded for its well-defined, innovative urban designs that age well and exhibit a special charm to both residential and commercial residents.

Holland's staff consists of licensed professional engineers and surveyors, engineer and survey technicians, a land planner and survey crews. The company uses state-of-the-art survey equipment, to include global positioning surveying equipment, and computer work stations with current and updated software applications for computer-aided design in engineering, surveying and administration.

Holland Engineering is committed to the professionalism demanded by our clients and the industry. The company continually strives to improve its quality of services with special attention to completeness and timeliness. To these ends, Holland Engineering fully supports and encourages its staff to become active members in professional organizations, to pursue continuing education and training, and to involve themselves in community organizations and activities.

Public and private clients have consistently turned to Holland Engineering for the services of skilled professionals who are committed to creating attractive designs for a variety of settings. For more information about the firm's extensive portfolio of civil engineering projects, contact President Mark Fields at Holland's Alexandria office.

Jane's Information Group

For more than 100 years, **Jane's Information Group** has been the world's foremost authority on defense information. Government officials, industry professionals and military personnel alike have come to rely on **Jane's** for the most accurate and impartial information available on the defense, intelligence, aerospace and transportation communities.

Jane's has developed a standard over the last century, as cited by Time Magazine, as having an "unrivaled reputation for accuracy and impartiality." From the very first edition of **Jane's Fighting Ships** in 1898 to the present day, **Jane's** has provided detailed information products and services some of which include **Jane's All the World's Aircraft** — the "bible" of the aviation industry — as well as **Jane's Defence Weekly** — considered by most to be the world's leading global defense magazine — and **Jane's Sentinel Security Assessments** — a geopolitical, regional risk and threat assessment service.

Over the years, **Jane's** has undergone continuous evolution to offer the most intelligent solutions that meet the changing information and technology requirements for today's professionals. The company now offers more than 380 sources of information in a variety of formats including hardcopy, CD-ROM, the Internet, Intranet and the advanced information delivery system, **Jane's Information Management System**.

Jane's daily e-mail service reaches governments, ministries, industry and media, providing real-time, comprehensive and technical information dealing with activities at the Pentagon and the Department of Defense and government contracting, in addition to memoranda and press releases. **Jane's** also offers specialized research reports, analyses and other custom services like **Jane's Consultancy Services Group** and **Jane's State & International Services Group**.

For the naval professional, **Jane's Fighting Ships**, **Jane's Naval Weapon Systems** and **Jane's Underwater Warfare Systems** provide the most extensive sources for technical specifications — with two new maritime publications this year, **Jane's Marine Propulsion** and **Jane's Asian and Pacific Rim Navies**. Other **Jane's** products include land-based information services such as **Jane's Armour and Artillery**, considered the authority on armored fighting vehicles and a new and timely reference work called **Jane's Chemical-Biological Defense Guidebook**. Also new to **Jane's** expanding list of products is **Jane's Air-Launched Weapons Imagery on CD-ROM** which is a comprehensive inventory of air-to-air and air-to-ground munitions including missiles, bomb and rockets — featuring photographs, cut-away drawings and rare video footage.

For more information on **Jane's** products, conferences and information services visit **Jane's** website at www.janes.com.

The Mark Winkler Company

For over 50 years, The Mark Winkler Company has been widely recognized as a leader in the metropolitan Washington, D.C. real estate community. During the five decades, The Mark Winkler Company has specialized in meeting the real estate needs of this important and challenging marketplace with the full scope of real estate services, including project development, property and asset management, leasing, and real estate and financial consulting. The Company's fundamental strength and stability have allowed it to achieve a steady and constant pattern of growth and expansion. Today, the Winkler portfolio consists of more than 10 million square feet of prime commercial and residential property and includes over $1 billion in assets under management throughout this region.

Winkler has successfully developed and managed properties ranging from corporate headquarters, both high-rise and mid-rise, to tilt-up warehouses and R&D facilities, and from garden apartments to thirty-story hotel structures. The Company's client base is broad and diverse, and includes large international organizations, financial institutions, Fortune 500 corporations, local and national companies of all sizes and individual family and corporate real estate owners and investors.

As long term owners of real estate, The Mark Winkler Company understands the need to preserve and enhance values. This commitment can be seen in Alexandria at Mark Center, a 350-acre mixed-use development, which remains one of the largest mixed-use projects inside the Capital Beltway.

Currently under construction is the Alexandria Association Campus at Mark Center which offers national trade and professional associations the opportunity to meet their space requirements within a campus setting, in a convenient location only five miles from Washington, D.C. The highest concentration of residential units in Alexandria can also be found at Mark Center, with over 5,000 rental apartments, including Millbrook at Mark Center, Winkler's newest luxury apartment community. Mark Center is also home to the world-class Radisson Plaza Hotel, one of the region's largest and most complete conference and business hotels.

The Mark Winkler Company is proud to have had its headquarters in Alexandria, Virginia for over 50 years, and looks forward to a continuing active presence in the Alexandria community.

Mount Comfort Cemetery

High above and overlooking the Potomac River, Mount Comfort Cemetery has been providing the finest available cemetery services to Northern Virginia residents for more than 50 years. The cemetery's mission is to demonstrate the highest degree of professionalism while assisting families at one of the most pivotal times in their lives.

The seasons at Mount Comfort reflect the full beauty of nature, from warm summer breezes to the brilliant cloak of autumn, from frost-tipped trees to bright spring flowers. The lush, landscaped 51-acre park offers traditional ground burial, mausoleum entombment, lawn crypts, private estates, private mausoleums, a cremation placement garden, cremation benches and estates.

An historic property, Mount Comfort and neighboring Mount Erin are two subdivisions of what originally was the Cleish estate, which was administered by George Washington. Founded on the banks of Great Hunting Creek by the sons of the Earl of Tankerville, the property was in the midst of many other colonial estates near Mount Vernon, around which revolved much of the important social and political activity in pre-Revolutionary days.

Mount Comfort's popular Sunrise Easter service, held in conjunction with Bethany Lutheran Church, has drawn hundreds of area residents for more than four decades. All offerings collected at the annual service are distributed to various local charities. Recent beneficiaries have included the Eleanor Kennedy Shelter, ASSIST Crisis Pregnancy Center of Fairfax, Mondloch House Family Shelter and Habitat for Humanity.

To learn more about how Mount Comfort can serve your family, please call 703-765-3800.

Society for Human Resource Management

The Society for Human Resource Management (SHRM) serves as the leading voice of the human resource profession. Founded in 1948, SHRM represents the interests of 90,000 members from around the globe.

The Society is a founding member of the North American Human Resource Management Association, and is also a founding member and Secretariat of the World Federation of Personnel Management Associations, which links human resource professionals worldwide.

In all, SHRM members are leaders who represent a broad cross-section of organizations, from Fortune 500 and 1000 companies to small businesses, from associations to government agencies. Its mission is to provide these decision makers with the tools and information necessary to ensure that an organization's most important asset — its people — are appropriately managed and respected.

In this vein, the Society provides its members with education and information services, conferences and seminars, government and media representation, online services and publications that equip human resource

professionals for their roles as leaders within their organizations. Organizations of all sizes and in every industry must understand the importance of human resource management as a motivating force for change as businesses redefine their relationships with employees, customers, stakeholders and competitors.

Founded by SHRM, the Human Resource Certification Institute (HRCI), promotes professional standards and recognizes those who master the body of knowledge that consti-

tutes the human resource profession. SHRM also established the SHRM Foundation, a non-profit organization that funds and supports research and educational programs directed toward developing and raising standards of performance in the human resource management field. The Institute for International Human Resources is also a division of SHRM and provides a forum for professionals involved in global human resource management.

A member of Alexandria's association community since 1984, SHRM employees actively support the city. Many of SHRM's 140 employees volunteer with the Alexandria United Way and the Carpenter's Shelter. These efforts demonstrate SHRM's numerous contributions to its professional community and the public community where SHRM staff live and work.

For these reasons, the Society for Human Resource Management is an association where people come first. For information about SHRM programs and services, visit their web site at http://www.SHRM.org.

Stevens Reed Curcio & Company

Founded by Greg Stevens, Stevens Reed Curcio & Company, Inc. is one of America's leading Republican media consulting companies for both political candidates and issue campaigns.

President Greg Stevens and partners Rick Reed and Paul Curcio have each worked in politics for over twenty years and are surrounded by one of the strongest teams of political professionals in the business. Since the formation of the firm in 1993, the firm has won more major statewide candidate campaigns than any other Republican media firm in the country, including four governors and five U.S. senators.

Stevens Reed Curcio & Company has also produced effective advertising for both corporations and issue coalitions across the country including the Health Insurance Agents of America, Blue Cross Blue Shield of New Jersey, Citizens for the Republic

Education Fund, Citizens for Responsible Workers' Compensation Reform, Maine Citizens for Jobs & Safety and the Virginia Department of Economic Development.

"Greg Stevens is the best person you could ever work with in this business. There is no doubt that Greg and his firm's creativity and unique abilities made a distinct difference in my coming from 38 points down to winning with 58% of the vote."
Governor George Allen (VA)

"Even our opponents and the hostile media conceded that the TV ads were masterful — a quantum leap above those of our three opponents."
Governor John Rowland (CT)

"In an industry filled with talented people and agencies, Greg Stevens and his company stand out...they make

each client — at least this client — feel like he is the only client they have."
Governor George Voinovich (OH)

"...the quality and creativity of the ads are the best in the business."
Senator Mitch McConnell (KY)

"When you run twice for the U.S. Senate, you get to know all the experts in the field. Greg Stevens and his staff really stood out."
Senator Gordon Smith (OR)

"I value Greg's advice and counsel and look forward to his help in my future efforts."
U.S. Representative Tom Davis (VA)

For more information about Stevens Reed Curcio & Company, please call 703-683-8326.

Time Life Inc.

Today, housed in its luxurious new world headquarters at Carlyle, Time Life Inc. seems to hold an almost permanent place in the Alexandria landscape.

But such has not always been the case.

For more than 16 years, from its incorporation in 1961, Time-Life Books operated quite successfully from its original home high in the famed Time & Life Building in New York.

With such landmark book series as *The Life World* and *Science Libraries* and *The Time Life Library of Art* and *Foods of the World* to its credit, the company ranked by 1970 as Time Inc.'s second most profitable publishing division — exceeded only by the 42-year-old TIME magazine.

As the company grew, Time Life's executives made the decision in 1976 to move out of New York, triggering a nationwide search for the optimal new location. Four months later, Alexandria, Virginia was announced as the clear winner. Based on its overall livability, as well as its proximity to the Library of Congress and other research facilities, Alexan-

dria more than answered the search committee's requirements.

Despite concerns that Time Life's younger Alexandria-based staff might lack the experience of their New York predecessors, sales results in 1977 — the company's first full year in Virginia – jumped to $215 million, a new corporate record.

Indeed, as the years passed, Time-Life Books found fertile ground along the banks of the Potomac. Cre-

ating dozens of best-selling series through the '80s, the transplanted company grew into the world's best-known mail order publisher.

How-to series such as *Home Repair and Improvement* and *Woodworking* provided advice and comfort for millions of ambitious do-it-yourselfers, while *Mysteries of the Unknown* made tales of the paranormal regular reading in America's living rooms. Other landmark series such as *World War II* and *The Civil War* remain required reading for students of military history.

Time Life also found new horizons beyond its core book business, launching divisions to create and sell high-quality music and home video collections – a move that soon met with enormous success.

As Time Life Inc. approaches the 21st century – and its 40th year in business – the company looks forward to a future even brighter than its lustrous past. A future filled with new opportunities to provide their customers with the most useful, most educational and most entertaining products money can buy.

Virginia-American Water Company

The Virginia-American Water Company has provided residents and businesses in Alexandria with safe, reliable drinking water for more than 150 years. The company is an established member of the community, dedicated to serving and supporting the families and businesses that call the city home.

Virginia-American is a subsidiary of the American Water Works Company, the largest investor-owned water utility in the U.S. Its 22 water utility subsidiaries serve a population of more than 7 million people in over 800 communities in 21 states. The American Water Works Company is nationally and internationally recognized as a leader in water quality, professional personnel, research, and laboratory facilities. In fact, the company works closely with the U.S. Environmental Protection Agency to develop nationwide safe drinking water standards.

Virginia-American's operations and facilities are regulated by the Virginia State Department of Health, the U.S. Environmental Protection Agency and the Virginia State Corporation Commission. Well-known for its high quality standards, the company tests for more contaminants, more often than regulations require. These tests are conducted both at its local testing facilities in Alexandria

and at the company's nationally recognized laboratory in Belleville, Illinois. As a result of its rigorous testing program, Virginia-American has developed a highly regarded reputation for responding to new state or federal regulations well before their implementation.

Reliability is another key component to the quality service furnished by Virginia-American. The company delivers approximately 15.5 million gallons of water a day throughout the City of Alexandria, and has the capacity to meet growth demands up to 26.3 million gallons a day. The company owns and maintains storage facilities with a total capacity of 23.7 million gallons.

Whether supporting national initiatives or providing reliable service to its many customers, Alexandria families and businesses alike can count on Virginia-American to continue providing safe, quality drinking water at a reasonable price.

Nonprofit
Associations
& Organizations

The National Association of Chain Drug Stores

NACDS historic headquarters building located on North Lee Street in Old Town, Alexandria.

From Alexandria to Your Neighborhood

Chain Community Pharmacy

The National Association of Chain Drug Stores (NACDS) has been located in an historic site in Old Town Alexandria, Virginia since 1980. The sense of community in Alexandria is unparalleled in the Washington metropolitan area.

NACDS is fortunate to work in a neighborhood whose citizens pride themselves on maintaining their rich history and sense of community while recognizing the value of business to the region.

The chain community pharmacy industry shares this recognition for the value of community. For more than a century, chain community pharmacies have been an indispensable part of community life in America. In neighborhoods, towns, and cities across this country, drug stores have been an important place for people to get news and information about pharmaceuticals and health care. The pharmacist has been a trusted and valued member of the "family," filling prescriptions and offering sound advice on the proper way to take medications.

NACDS is committed to this community and provides support to local business and civic organizations such as the Alexandria Chamber of Commerce, the Alexandria Symphony, and The Campagna Center.

NACDS' members are equally committed to providing all communities with the finest health care delivery infrastructure in the world. Our members are at the forefront of technology, choice, convenience and patient information, and have much to offer your community today and in the future.

A Message from the President and CEO

Ronald L. Ziegler, President and Chief Executive Officer, National Association of Chain Drug Stores.

Message from the President and Chief Executive Officer

We welcome this opportunity to acquaint you with the National Association of Chain Drug Stores and the important industry we represent...chain owned and operated community pharmacy.

Founded in 1933, NACDS was created to assist traditional chain drug stores in complying with federal laws and regulations which impact the business of pharmacy. Today, the mission of NACDS has grown dramatically.

NACDS plays an important role in shaping federal health care policy. We are at the forefront of developing initiatives that enable our members to meet the realities of the rapidly changing health care marketplace. NACDS fulfills its mission by offering a variety

of services that build a favorable legislative, regulatory and business climate in which member companies continue to meet growing customer needs and expectations.

With a cost-effective distribution system, chain community pharmacies provide access to many valued goods and services for most Americans. No matter where you live in the United States, chances are that there is a community pharmacy in your neighborhood... meeting your community's health needs and providing important health care services.

In addition to traditional drug stores, NACDS members now include supermarkets and mass merchants which operate pharmacies. Collectively, these retail establishments are what we call "chain community pharmacy."

In all, there are over 30,000 chain

Ronald L. Ziegler, NACDS President and CEO, and President Clinton at a White House Bill Signing Ceremony.

The pharmacist is a highly accessible, trusted and valued leader in the community.

owned and operated community pharmacies with annual sales totaling more than $125 billion, including prescription drugs, over-the-counter medications, and health and beauty aids. Chain community pharmacies fill approximately 60% of the more than 2.6 billion prescriptions dispensed annually in the United States and provide professional practice settings for 88,000 pharmacists.

NACDS also has more than 1,300 associate member companies that supply goods and services to the industry and 70 international members from 22 countries.

Your chain community pharmacist is available to talk with you about your particular health care needs. We invite you to stop in.

Ronald L. Ziegler

Chain Community Pharmacy:

Valued Services Offered by Your Community Pharmacy

For the last eight years Americans have rated the honesty and ethical standards of pharmacists highest among twenty-six occupations surveyed by the Gallup Poll. In many communities pharmacists are the most accessible health care professionals, available to the consumer on evenings, weekends, holidays, and sometimes around the clock.

As your community health resource center, chain community pharmacies provide cost-effective, high quality patient care. Following are a few of the important benefits they offer the public.

- *Counsel patients*

Patient counseling is a critical component of pharmacists' care. The pharmacist is always available to discuss with the patient how and when to take a medication, and what to do if a dose is missed. Pharmacists also discuss possible side effects, proper storage,

One of the more than 30,000 chain pharmacies offering counseling services to consumers.

and when to contact your doctor about problems.

- *Screen prescriptions*

Pharmacists review every prescription to ensure the medication is prescribed in the appropriate dosage.

- *Review patient profiles*

Patient records are reviewed to identify allergies, potential interactions with other prescription and over-the-counter medications, duplicate prescriptions, or other adverse consequences.

- *Correct potential problems*

Should the pharmacist detect any potential for adverse consequences, or have questions or concerns about the appropriateness of a particular

medication, the pharmacist may contact the physician to discuss and resolve a potential problem.

- *Dispense medication*

The pharmacist prepares the medication prescribed in accordance with the physician's instructions, and in some cases "compounds" a special medication required by the doctor. Pharmacists also label prescriptions to identify the contents and, when necessary, affix extra labels with specific instructions for proper use.

- *Monitor progress*

Pharmacists may also monitor the patients' progress with prescribed drug therapy to ensure that they are taking their medication properly, refilling their medication on time and are not experiencing side effects. Pharmacists will refer patients back to their physician if necessary.

Chain pharmacies have a long history of meeting consumer needs for many products and services beyond medications.

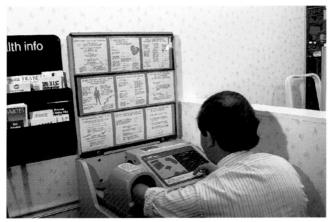

Chain pharmacies provide many health monitoring services such as this blood pressure screening.

Always a Part of Your Neighborhood

Specialized health care services similar to this Diabetic Center are now offered by some chain pharmacies.

Services Provided By Pharmacists Frequently Include The Following:

- Advice on over-the-counter products

- Health screening programs such as hypertension, diabetes and cholesterol

- Wellness programs such as smoking cessation, diet and exercise

- Patient education

- Drug abuse prevention

- Education of other health professionals

- Specialty practices servicing patients with AIDS, diabetes, and other diseases

- A full range of medications and compounded specialty medications

Though the store front has changed, chain pharmacies continue their tradition as a convenient and accessible health center.

- 24-hour store hours

- Assistance with insurance claims

- Convenient drive-up window service

At a time when consumers increasingly look for value-added services and cost-effective, results oriented health care, your chain community pharmacy is working hard to meet your needs.

Questions Your Community Pharmacist Will Answer for You

Chain community pharmacies continue to work hard to meet the changing needs of their customers. To achieve this goal the industry has expanded its role in providing health services and educating consumers about pharmaceutical products and health issues.

To meet the customers' need for convenient, easy access to pharmacy and other consumer products and services, pharmacists are providing new and valued services to their patients and the community.

Many chain pharmacies such as this one now offer 24-hour and drive-thru service.

American Association of Colleges of Pharmacy

AACP-Advancing Pharmaceutical Education's Agenda

Founded in 1900, the American Association of Colleges of Pharmacy (AACP) is the national organization representing pharmaceutical education in the United States. The mission of the Association is to represent and be an advocate for all segments of the academic community in the profession of pharmacy. That community is composed of 79 colleges and schools with pharmacy programs accredited by the American Council on Pharmaceutical Education. There are approximately 33,000 professional degree students, 2,900 students enrolled in graduate studies, and approximately 3,000 full-time faculty at the nation's pharmacy schools.

All 79 schools of pharmacy are institutional members of AACP. Each school has two votes in the AACP House of Delegates, the body which establishes policy for pharmaceutical education in the United States. Faculty may also be individual members of AACP, entitling them to receive a number of services and to participate

in the various activities of the Association. Nearly two-thirds of all full-time faculty choose to become members of AACP, a high percentage of individual membership for a national organization. AACP enjoys the widespread support of the community it represents and there is a high degree of faculty participation within its committees, academic sections, and special interest groups.

AACP-Serving Its Members

In addition to the full range of expected member services, including journal and newsletter publishing, professional and educational meetings, seminars and a newly developed home page on the World Wide Web, AACP offers comprehensive programmatic activities to assist faculty in their important work of educating the nation's future pharmacists and pharmaceutical students. Pharmacists, as medication use experts in all health care settings, as educators and consultants, and as researchers, are essential to the nation's health. U.S. colleges and schools of pharmacy are meeting the challenge of preparing these professionals for this important work.

AACP relocated its headquarters to Alexandria, Virginia from Bethesda, Maryland in 1984 in response to the city's major initiatives to attract organizations representing professional and technical groups. The Association built its headquarters at 1426 Prince Street and is one of several organizations representing various interests in pharmacy and the pharmaceutical sciences located in Alexandria.

Stabler-Leadbeater Apothecary Museum

Founded in 1792, The Stabler-Leadbeater Apothecary Shop's one hundred and forty-one years of operating history is completely documented. Our archival material...in excess of 150 cubic feet of records... confirms that the Museum is on the forefront of Alexandria's interpretive history. The Shop's history not only includes service to Martha Washington and family, but it also encompasses four wars, rampaging epidemics and the remarkable history of founder, Edward Stabler. Says The Library of Virginia, "the collection appears to be one of the most impressive... archives extant."

Edward Stabler's historical legacy is one of the contemporary man. In 1816, Quaker Stabler protested the country's "internal traffic in people of color." By 1819, he was testifying before Congress regarding the inhuman treatment of the American Indian.

Many of the firm's customers were famous...Drs. James Craik and Elisha Cullen Dick, James Monroe and Bvt. Colonel Robert E. Lee. More interesting, perhaps, is the Shop's community clientele...ordinary

names...family names...many Alexandrians still recognize today.

The Museum's valuable collection is not limited to its archives. The collection includes, besides furnishings and fixtures, pharmaceutical equipment and herbs. Pharmacognosists report that our Herb Collection may hold many important scientific secrets.

Our history spans the centuries. We celebrate the legacy of George Washington; the era of natural prod-

ucts in pharmacy and founder Edward Stabler's scholarship. For many, the most interesting history is that which explains the city of Alexandria. Yet, we are able to offer the corporate community so much more.

The Apothecary Museum is now supporting research into our early history. We can accurately trace the evolution of the prescription form; changes in medical technology; narcotics control, as well as the 1920's prohibition of medicinal alcohol. The Apothecary Museum is Alexandria's only historical science museum.

The Stabler-Leadbeater Apothecary Shop is a unique reminder of the period when manufacturing, wholesaling and dispensing of medicines were combined in a single enterprise. The Apothecary Museum is Alexandria's only museum with an original collection in its original location. It is located at 105-107 S. Fairfax Street, Alexandria, Virginia 22314. (703-836-3713) Visit with us!

The Stabler-Leadbeater Apothecary Museum gratefully acknowledges the American Association of Colleges of Pharmacy for its generous contribution of this page.

Alexandria City Public Schools

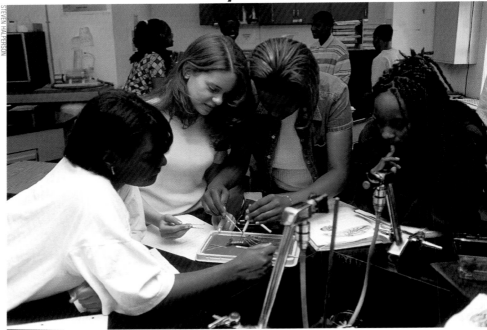

The mission of the Alexandria City Public Schools is to provide every K-12 student the opportunity for a quality education. To this end, Alexandria schools have implemented a multiple component educational program that is responsive to identified individual student needs for enrichment, practice, remediation, literacy and achievement. In addition, the district supports an extensive adult education program.

Through its highly successful Technology Initiative, Alexandria schools are retooling to teach children the skills they will need for life in the 21st century. This four-year initiative is equipping Alexandria classrooms and libraries with state-of-the-art computer and video equipment and training Alexandria teachers in its use. Alexandria classrooms are wired via fiber optic cable to the Internet through computers located in each room, a connection provided by Jones Communications.

Alexandria maintains high academic standards. Eight out of ten students at T.C. Williams, Alexandria's nationally recognized comprehensive high school, pursue post-secondary education. Those who select a vocational education gain experience in programs that are well-regarded and supported by the business community.

Alexandria is one of the few school systems in the region with a complete full-day kindergarten program. Alexandria is also known for its comprehensive special education program and its Spanish Immersion program for grades 1 through 8. Of special note is its Primary Initiative, a commitment to parents and the community that all students will have reading and mathematics skills at or above grade level by the end of the second grade.

Alexandria schools provide a true international experience, with students representing 64 birth nations and speaking 44 native languages. Local support for education is strong, including 50 school-business partners, over 50,000 volunteer hours each year in the schools, and $175,000 raised annually for scholarships to Alexandria graduates through The Scholarship Fund of Alexandria.

Special thanks to those whose generosity made this page possible: Bell Atlantic, Colonial Parking, Computing Analysis Corporation, Crestar Bank, Mark Winkler Company, Metropolitan Airports Authority, Printing Industries of America, Pardoe/Graham, Radio Free Italy/Mango Mike's, Simpson Development Company, Inc., and Time Life, Inc.

Club Managers
Association of America

Incorporated in 1927, the Club Managers Association of America (CMAA) is the professional association for managers of the leading private membership clubs in the United States and abroad. CMAA offers continuing education, executive career services, a national trade magazine, *Club Management*, and a public web site on the Internet with a private, members only section, ClubNet, to its more than 5,000 members. CMAA's budget is $4.5 million. The staff numbers 28. There are 50 chapters both in the United States and internationally.

the advancement of the club management profession. The Foundation sponsors research, funds education programs, provides financial assistance to educational institutions and awards scholarships to both club managers and outstanding students interested in the club management profession.

CMAA also collects and disseminates information on the little-known club industry. For example, clubs employ more than 237,000 people, and club payrolls equal $3.1 billion. The average club spends $1.26 million in the local community. Overall, club operations generate $3.6 billion for state economies around the country.

The objectives of the Association are to promote and advance friendly relations between and among persons connected with the management of clubs and other associations of similar character; to encourage the education and advancement of its members; and to assist club officers and members, through their managers, to secure the utmost in efficient and successful operations.

CMAA lives up to its motto of "professionalism in club management" through its Lifetime Profes-

sional Development Program. As the educational arm of the Association, the Club Management Institute is the primary entity responsible for this mission.

The Association also takes great pride in its certification program. Begun in 1965, the Certified Club Manager (CCM) designation is known as "the hallmark of professionalism in club management."

The Club Foundation, the charitable arm of the Association, supports

economies around the country.

Clubs are more than just considerable contributors to local economies, however. They also support their communities through a spirit of generosity that is a model for the private sector. Clubs raise an average of more than $123 million each year for charities. CMAA individual members and entire chapters participate in the Association's annual, nationwide community service campaign-Clubs Collecting for Communities.

The George Washington University

Since its founding in 1821, The George Washington University has been one of the nation's leading institutions of higher education. Today, GW consists of seven schools, all of which are pioneers in their fields.

The George Washington University attracts some of the best and brightest students from across the nation and around the world. With its world-renowned faculty and main campus located in the heart of the Nation's Capital, GW offers access to a wide range of outstanding educational and professional resources.

Today, The Office of Academic Development and Continuing Education provides a wide choice of graduate and certificate programs conveniently scheduled throughout the Washington metropolitan area to meet the needs of busy working professionals.

The Alexandria Graduate Educa-tion Center, located at 1775 Duke Street adjacent to the King Street Metro Station in Alexandria, is one of GW's eight off-campus locations. This spacious facility opened in the fall of 1996 and offers eight popular Master's Degree programs in engineering and education.

Classes are conveniently scheduled on weekday evening and weekends to meet the time limits of busy working adults. The Center is easily accessible with plenty of safe, convenient parking. Registration is handled by touchtone phone and textbook purchases are available by mail.

The high admissions standards and distinguished faculty for which The George Washington University is so respected create a challenging classroom environment for achievers who strive for excellence. The knowledge, skill and contacts gained over the course of enrollment benefit students for years to come.

The Alexandria Graduate Education Center is also the site of the Alexandria Small Business Development Center. Working with existing and potential businesses in Alexandria, the SBDC provides one-on-one counseling, training and information and referral services, in addition to specialized business planning for new and existing small businesses in the Northern Virginia area. Because of its tie to the University, students at the Alexandria Graduate Education Center frequently work with the SBDC and area businesses on special projects.

For more information about the professional and business opportunities offered by George Washington University's Alexandria Graduate Education Center, please call 703-299-0197.

National Association of Temporary and Staffing Services

The recognized voice of the staffing services industry, the National Association of Temporary and Staffing Services represents over 1,600 member companies with over 13,000 offices, and 82 affiliate chapters in the United States, Washington, D.C. and Puerto Rico. Its member companies serve both Fortune 500 and 1000 companies and small businesses, providing essential staffing support to every sector of the U.S. economy.

NATSS member companies provide businesses with ready access to a wide range of skilled workers – from industrial to clerical, professional and executive – who can provide the adjunct support necessary to keep America competitive. As a result of market forces created by new and emerging technologies, for example, the staffing industry is a valued source of highly skilled employees.

Founded in 1966 as the Institute of Temporary Services, the mission and scope of the organization has changed markedly in the past three decades to reflect the exponential growth in the staffing services indus-

try. Today, NATSS members represent the full range of staffing services, from professional employer services and managed services (often called "outsourcing") to payrolling and placement services, as well as temporary-to-full-time and long-term staffing services.

NATSS member companies offer temporary employees multiple opportunities for valuable training and on-the-job experience and, as such, annually invests hundreds of millions of

dollars in educational programs. The staffing industry also serves as a useful entry way through which millions have transitioned from under-employment or unemployment to full-time jobs or flexible career opportunities.

As part of its efforts to draw positive awareness of the many economic contributions of the staffing services industry to business and local communities, NATSS sponsors National Temporary Help Week each October in conjunction with its member companies. It also operates the NATSS Foundation, a 501(c)(3) organization that supports the association's business-education partnership, Preparing Youth For Industry (PYI). PYI builds awareness about job preparation and skills enhancement among "at-risk" high school students.

Visit the NATSS website at http://www.natss.org for more information about the association's public relations and legislative advocacy, education and informational programs.

Quality of Life

City of Alexandria

Alexandria City Hall and Market Square. (Photo by Anna M. Frame)

Alexandria, Virginia, is an historic City with an exciting future. Founded by Scottish and English merchants in 1749, Alexandria occupies 16 square miles and is home to 118,000 residents, making it the largest city in the suburbs of Washington, D.C. Alexandria will celebrate its 250th anniversary in 1999.

Located on the Potomac River across from the nation's capital, Alexandria is a center of business and commerce. Employers, including Time Life, Inc. and PBS, make Alexandria a major job center, with over 84,000 people employed in technology, associations, government, retail, and professional services. Alexandrians enjoy easy access to National Airport, Metrorail and Metrobus, Amtrak, Virginia Railway Express and the City's DASH bus system.

The "Home Town of George Wash-ington and Robert E. Lee," Alexandria is rich in historic, educational and cultural resources. In Old Town Alexandria, more than 1,000 historic structures are preserved as private homes, shops, restaurants, art galleries, and museums. The City offers public, private and parochial schools, and higher learning institutions. A state-of-the-art central library will open in 1999. Alexandrians also enjoy the Alexandria Symphony Orchestra, the Torpedo Factory Art Center, City museums and recreation centers and over 800 acres of parks.

Alexandria's City government is widely recognized for providing high quality services and innovations in technology, human services, and public safety. The City is governed by a City Council, including the Mayor, Vice Mayor and five other City Council Members. An appointed City Manager oversees the City's day-to-day op-erations. Alexandria's community policing initiatives reduced serious crime to a 27-year low in 1996, and first-class fire and emergency medical services make Alexandria among the best served cities in the nation. An All-America City, Alexandria is one of only 30 U.S. cities and counties with triple-A bond ratings from both of Wall Street's major credit rating agencies. The City cooperates with neighboring jurisdictions through the Metropolitan Washington Council of Governments and other regional agencies. To promote economic development and tourism, the City participates in such public-private partnerships as the Alexandria Economic Development Partnership, the Alexandria Convention and Visitors Association, the Potomac West Alliance, and the Eisenhower Avenue Partnership. The City operates a web site at (http://ci.alexandria.va.us/alexandria.html).

Inova Mount Vernon Hospital

Inova Mount Vernon Hospital is a 235-bed community hospital located a few miles from the famous estate of George Washington. Serving the health care needs of Northern Virginia since 1976, Inova Mount Vernon Hospital provides all acute care medical and surgical services (with the exception of obstetrics), including cancer, emergency, psychiatric, cardiac rehabilitation, breast health, hyperbaric oxygen and dialysis care. The hospital is home to the nationally recognized Inova Rehabilitation Center and the Inova Joint Replacement Center.

In 1996, Inova received the highest rating, accreditation with commendation, given by the Joint Commission on Accreditation of Healthcare Organizations (JCAHO), the national hospital accreditation organization. This is an achievement reached by less than five percent of all hospitals surveyed by JCAHO.

Inova Mount Vernon takes pride in the expertise and experience of its dedicated staff of physicians, nurses and other health care professionals who provide the highest quality care to our patients. For the community, the hospital also offers wellness classes and support groups. In concern for employees, Inova Mount Vernon Hospital has its own fully accredited child care center for children of hospital staff.

In response to the fundamental changes in the health care environment, especially the shift in focus from inpatient to outpatient care, Inova Mount Vernon Hospital has undertaken a major restructuring and expansion project, Mount Vernon 2000 (MV 2000). This initiative is the culmination of many years of planning by diverse groups vested in the future of the Mount Vernon community. MV 2000 expands facilities for outpatient services, increases space for new technologies and positions the hospital for significant growth in its two centers of excellence: rehabilitation and orthopedics.

Inova Mount Vernon Hospital is affiliated with Inova Health System, a comprehensive not-for-profit health care system based in Northern Virginia consisting of hospitals and other health services including home care, nursing homes, mental health services, family practices, wellness classes and free-standing emergency and urgent care centers. Our mission is to provide services that improve the health of all individuals in our community regardless of their ability to pay.

Executive Club Suites

610 Bashford Lane • Ph. 703-739-2582 • Fax 703-739-4950 • www.dcexeclub.com

The Executive Club Suites carries on the ancient and honorable hotel traditions of warmth and hospitality. The Georgian architecture, antique brick and gracious carriage house entrance welcomes you. The lobby is in the classic European style: friendly, intimate and immaculately appointed. And our entire staff is well-versed in the fine art of making you feel comfortably at home. Beginning with our Guest Services Representative, we change what a hotel does by changing how we do it-with promptness, courtesy and friendly personal attention. We serve you with pleasure and it shows.

At Executive Club Suites, your suite is actually a full-sized apartment home of at least 650 square feet. Chock full of every amenity, it's no wonder our guests refer to us as their Home Away From Home. Each apartment is complete with a living room, modern kitchen, separate dining area and private bedroom and bath-all with elegant Queen Anne furnishings.

Our guests feel right at home in our living rooms, each with remote-control televisions with cable and Home Box Office, gracious wing-back chairs and a queen-size sleep sofa. Our modern kitchens are complete with full-sized refrigerators and mi-

crowaves, stove top, coffee makers, pots and pans, dinnerware and flatware for four, and cooking utensils. Don't feel like cooking? Alexandria restaurants are among the very best, offering something for everyone's taste and budget. Many local restaurants also provide delivery service for those evenings when you feel like staying in.

The Executive Club's private bedrooms are spacious and beautifully appointed, allowing you to sleep comfortably in our queen-size beds. A second remote-control television in each bedroom allows you to rest comfortably while watching the news or

Vernon. And, you and your family will enjoy relaxing around our seasonal outdoor swimming pool from Memorial Day throughout the summer.

That's not all. Executive Club Suites offers free continental breakfast on weekday mornings. Wake to the smell of fresh coffee, juice, pastries, danish and seasonal fresh fruit. End your work day by joining us in our Club Room for our guest reception; over complimentary beverages and appetizers you'll meet old friends and make new ones.

your favorite show. Each suite also has two telephones.

While we offer one bedroom, one bedroom with den and two bedroom suites, guests are always welcome-and for no extra charge. And there's plenty of room (and privacy) for cribs or rollaway beds too.

The Executive Club staff and facilities offer the comforts and conveniences of a luxury hotel but at reasonable government per diem and corporate rates. There is a 24-hour switchboard message service, voice mail, daily maid service and laundry and valet pick up and delivery. Coin-operated laundry facilities are also available.

Our fully equipped Health Club, complete with treadmills,

stairclimbers, exercise bikes and Universal weight equipment, makes it easy to squeeze in your workout. For runners and walkers, the Old Town Executive Club is adjacent to the 18-mile George Washington Memorial bike path, which gently follows the Potomac River south to Mount

Knowing that executives on the road often require access to business services, our Computer Room is available to our guests 24 hours a day. The room is equipped with a PC, printer

and recent versions of commonly used software packages, including Windows, MS-DOS and WordPerfect. Our offerings are certainly not limited to these packages, however, as Executive Club Suites continues to upgrade the Computer Room on a regular basis. For those who use lap top computers, in-room modem ports are provided on a request basis. Fax services are also available in the hotel.

For your convenience, we also offer meeting facilities. Our 500+ square foot Hunt Room is perfectly designed for a very successful small business meeting. It is the ideal training room, and is designed to accommodate up to 30 attendees.

Our Board Room, at 200+ square feet, is a beautifully appointed executive conference room with a cherry conference table and rich, comfortable chairs. At the Old Town Alexandria Executive Club, the Board Room is designed to accommodate 12 to 14 persons, and at our Rosslyn Executive Club, up to 20 persons. Audio equipment is available for rent at a nominal cost. We will work with the caterer of your choice, or can provide catering to assure a successful, flawless meeting.

For groups that require a larger meeting space, Executive Club Suites is prepared to host 'off-site' meetings. Please contact our Sales Department for more information.

And during your stay, whether you are planning a small reception or a family get-together, Executive Club's in-house caterer can provide for your every need. We invite you to speak with our Sales Director about your specific needs.

Our focus is on providing you with the most comfortable, productive environment possible. In addition to ample free parking, we offer dependable shuttle transportation service to National Airport, the Metro rail station, and other selected destinations. And talk about location! The Executive Club Suites are convenient to major highways and area centers of business. In addition to Executive

Club locations in Rosslyn and Arlington near the Navy Annex and the Pentagon, our Old Town Alexandria hotel is minutes from Washington, D.C., the Pentagon, and other area military and contractor installations.

Guests at our Old Town Alexandria location are visiting one of America's oldest seaports, which offers exquisite examples of early Americana. Whether you take a formal tour of the city or simply stroll down the quaint cobblestone streets, Old Town is a bit of living history that everyone should experience. Not to mention the attractions of our Nation's Capital, just across the Potomac River.

As for dining and entertainment, you can enjoy everything from symphony concerts to foot-stompin' country fiddling, from fine French cuisine to batter-fried American catfish. Old Town provides unforgettable evenings of fun and festivity in a charming, waterfront setting. In fact, when people come here on business they have so much fun that they bring their entire families back to the Executive Club Suites for vacation. Our cheerful atmosphere will make your visit to the Washington area one of the most enjoyable trips you will ever make.

We are proud of the professional, friendly, responsive service that our Executive Club staff consistently provides. We invite you to visit our Club Room, where our walls are lined with comments from just a few of the many who have found that Executive Club truly is a place where they can be at home while away from home.

The Executive Club offers a great deal of space, comfort, service and convenience. But our suites don't cost a great deal of money (and they include just about every amenity you can think of). To the contrary, our rates are well below what many people pay for a comparable hotel room. We also offer short- and long-term leases. Call us for reservations today at: 1-800-535-CLUB (2582) or locally at 703-739-2582 ext. 1405.

Northern Virginia Community College

The Alexandria Campus of Northern Virginia Community College (NOVA) is one of five campuses serving the northern Virginia area. NOVA is the largest institution of higher education in the Commonwealth of Virginia, enrolling more than 60,000 credit students each year in over 130 programs of study. Tuition rates for in-state students are among the most affordable in the area, making NOVA an exceptional educational value.

Like all NOVA campuses, Alexandria reflects the community that surrounds it. The campus offers a cosmopolitan atmosphere and international flavor, since the student population is drawn from a variety of cultural backgrounds. More than 17,000 individuals enroll in credit classes at this location, which includes both occupational/technical and college-transfer curricula. Thousands more participate in non-credit classes and community education activities. The campus also has a strong workforce development presence with area businesses, industries and military operations.

Course offerings in the areas of science, liberal arts, information systems technology, early childhood development and business — including a major in international business — are offered here, and an extensive English as a second language (ESL) program is also in place. The Alexandria Campus also boasts a strong fine arts program, where students can select offerings in computer graphics, photography and music. The campus's Tyler Gallery rotates exhibits that showcase the works of student and professional artists.

Plans for the construction of the Rachel M. Schlesinger Concert Hall and Arts Center on the Alexandria Campus are well underway. Named by its major donor, former U.S. Secretary of Defense James R. Schlesinger in memory of his wife, this building will be the cultural centerpiece for Alexandria's artistic community and will be available for performances by both the Arlington and Alexandria symphonies. Privately funded, the 46,000 square foot structure will include a 1,000 seat concert hall, art gallery, forum, seminar rooms, and an "arts incubator" where small budding arts groups will be offered a base of operation.

Northern Virginia Community College is located at 3001 N. Beauregard Street, between Route 7 and Seminary Road, just west of Interstate 395. The campus may be reached by Metro Bus, and there is ample parking for visitors, students, faculty and staff. For information, please call the Alexandria Campus at 703-845-6200.

The Restaurant Cruise Ship Dandy and The Potomac Riverboat Company

The Restaurant Cruise Ship Dandy

The DANDY was designed to cruise under the dramatic, low arched bridges and cruises past our Nation's monuments all the way to Georgetown and back to beautiful, historic Old Town Alexandria.

The DANDY is world renown for excellent food and service in a truly elegant atmosphere. The wall to wall windows, plush acanthus patterned carpeting, crisp linens, prints of Renoir, Monet and Beraud, and a marble dance floor give the room an Old World look. She is a climate-controlled, all weather restaurant. Cold weather cruises can be especially fun; guests like to gather around the antique wood-burning parlour stove and drink hot alcoholic and non-alcoholic beverages.

The DANDY pioneered fine dining on the water and has eighteen years of successful operating experience and is a woman-owned and operated business. The DANDY is available for breakfast, brunch, lunch mid-day, dinner or midnight-dance cruises for tow, a small group or as many as 200. Private charters, group discounts, and gift certificates are available. For information and reservations, call 703-683-6076.

The DANDY, nestled in historic, beautiful Old Town Alexandria, affords you the convenience of a huge public parking lot adjacent to and with a gate that opens to the Dandy's docking area. The quaint old-fashioned wooden pier with red carpeting, and huge flower-filled baskets lining both sides of the walk-way seem to transport you from the hustle-bustle of the city to the quietly exciting waterfront. The long benches along the depth of the pier welcome you to sit and enjoy the river sights before and after your cruise aboard the DANDY.

Potomac Riverboat Company

Potomac Riverboat Company offers a fleet of vessels for business and social entertaining. **The Cherry Blossom** is an

authentic split stern wheeler designed and created for private entertaining. Her two interior salons are heated and air-conditioned for year-round comfort and an open third deck offers spectacular views of the greater Washington Skyline.

Enjoy a relaxing, sightseeing tour aboard one of the company's smaller vessels: **the Matthew Hayes** offers a 90-minute cruise of Washington's monuments, such as the Lincoln and Jefferson Memorials, the Washington Monument, and the Kennedy Center; **the Miss Christin** offers a scenic cruise to Mount Vernon, home of George Washington. Upon arrival at the Estate, a land tour is available of the grounds, gardens, and museums; **the Admiral Tilp** offers a 40-minute tour of Alexandria's history as a seaport town.

For information about sightseeing tours and private charters aboard any of these vessels, please call 703-684-0580.

Index

Corporate Profiles in Excellence Index